KU-161-452

Oxford Modern Britain   SERIES EDITOR JOHN SCOTT

Women and Voting in Modern Britain

WITHDRAWN

LIVERPOOL JMU LIBRARY

3 1111 00735 9365

The *Oxford Modern Britain* series comprises authoritative introductory books on all aspects of the social structure of modern Britain. Lively and accessible, the books will be the first point of reference for anyone interested in the state of contemporary Britain. They will be invaluable to those taking courses in the social sciences.

Oxford Modern Britain

Women and Work in Modern Britain

Rosemary Crompton

OXFORD UNIVERSITY PRESS
1997

Oxford University Press, Great Clarendon Street, Oxford OX2 6DP
Oxford New York
Athens Auckland Bangkok Bogota Bombay
Buenos Aires Calcutta Cape Town Dar es Salaam
Delhi Florence Hong Kong Istanbul Karachi
Kuala Lumpur Madras Madrid Melbourne
Mexico City Nairobi Paris Singapore
Taipei Tokyo Toronto Warsaw
and associated companies in
Berlin Ibadan

Oxford is a trade mark of Oxford University Press

Published in the United States
by Oxford University Press Inc., New York

© Rosemary Crompton 1997

All rights reserved. No part of this publication may be reproduced,
stored in a retrieval system, or transmitted, in any form or by any
means, without the prior permission in writing of Oxford
University Press. Within the UK, exceptions are allowed in respect
of any fair dealing for the purpose of research or private study, or
criticism or review, as permitted under the Copyright, Designs and
Patents Act, 1988, or in the case of reprographic reproduction in
accordance with the terms of the licences issued by the Copyright
Licensing Agency. Enquiries concerning reproduction outside these
terms and in other countries should be sent to the Rights
Department, Oxford University Press, at the address above

This book is sold subject to the condition that it shall not, by way
of trade or otherwise, be lent, re-sold, hired out or otherwise
circulated without the publisher's prior consent in any form of
binding or cover other than that in which it is published and
without a similar condition including this condition being
imposed on the subsequent purchaser

British Library Cataloguing in Publication Data
Data available

Library of Congress Cataloging in Publication Data
Crompton, Rosemary.
Women and work in modern Britain / Rosemary Crompton.
(Oxford modern Britain)
Includes bibliographical references.
1. Women—Employment—Great Britain. 2. Work and family—Great
Britain. 3. Women employees—Great Britain. I. Title.
II. Series.
HD6135.C76 1997
331.4'0941—dc21 97-12931
CIP
ISBN 0-19-878096-6 ISBN 0-19-878097-4 (Pbk.)

1 3 5 7 9 10 8 6 4 2

Typeset by Best-set Typesetter Ltd., Hong Kong
Printed in Great Britain
on acid-free paper by
Biddles Ltd., Guildford and King's Lynn

Foreword

The Oxford Modern Britain series is designed to fill a major gap in the available sociological sources on the contemporary world. Each book will provide a comprehensive and authoritative overview of the major issues for students at all levels. They are written by acknowledged experts in their fields, and should be standard sources for many years to come.

Each book focuses on contemporary Britain, but the relevant historical background is always included, and a comparative context is provided. No society can be studied in isolation from other societies and the globalized context of the contemporary world, but a detailed understanding of a particular society can both broaden and deepen sociological understanding. These books will be exemplars of empirical study and theoretical understanding.

Books in the series are intended to present information and ideas in a lively and accessible way. They will meet a real need for source books in a wide range of specialized course, in 'Modern Britain' and 'Comparative Sociology' courses, and in integrated introductory courses. They have been written with the newcomer and general reader in mind, and they meet the genuine need in the informed public for accurate and up-to-date discussion and sources.

John Scott
Series Editor

Acknowledgements

I would like to thank both Gerald Crompton and Fiona Harris, who have read the first drafts of several chapters in this book and who have made useful suggestions for improvement. Fiona Harris generated Figures for Chapter 2 and 4. Finally, the ESRC funded some of the research (R000235617) which fed into discussions in Chapters 3 and 5.

Contents

List of Figures

List of Tables

LIVERPOOL
JOHN MOORES UNIVERSITY
AVRIL ROBARTS LRC
TITHEBARN STREET
LIVERPOOL L2 2ER
TEL. 0151 231 4022

Introduction

The increase in the number of married women going out to work has been one of the major social changes to have taken place in Britain since the Second World War. After the war (i.e. during the 1940s), the majority of women (including married women), who had been mobilized as an essential part of the war effort, returned to domestic life. The network of state day nurseries for small children, which had been set up in order to allow their mothers to work, was closed down. Theories of childcare and development formulated during the 1950s emphasized, above all, the absolute requirement for constant attention from the mother for the first years of a child's life (Riley 1983), supplying a moral justification, if one was needed, for the exclusion of mothers from the labour force. However, as there was in fact a labour shortage, many women nevertheless continued in employment, usually in part-time work, which was 'officially' encouraged.

Thus the numbers of women going 'out to work' carried on rising, even if only gradually; and by the 1960s it was apparent that this trend would continue. The 1960s were also years of political ferment, in which social norms were being transformed with some rapidity. Campaigns for Civil Rights for Blacks in the US were closely followed by the development of 'second-wave' feminism (Friedan 1965). 'Second-wave' feminism went beyond the idea of a formal equality for women, such as the right to vote and hold political office, and to be treated equally with men in terms of the law, to argue for a real equality with men which included equal access to all areas of employment and political life as well as the unpacking and transformation of stereotypical ideas governing relationships between men and women—hence the slogan that 'the personal is the political'.

Much of the discussion and activity around 'second-wave' feminism was directly concerned with the world of paid employment and access to it. This is hardly surprising as, for the vast majority of people, paid employment is the means to an independent life. The majority of

1

women did not (and still do not) have access to jobs which pay enough money for them to be able to live independently (assuming that they wish to do so). Men tend to predominate in the best-paid jobs (which are also often the most secure, with good employment conditions such as pensions), and women predominate in the worst-paid jobs. Furthermore, the fact that a woman's major responsibility was and is assumed to be that of the home and family (if she has one) means that the majority of women spent long periods of their adult lives either out of the labour force, or working part-time.

Today the situation is changing; but the scenario sketched out above provides the starting-point for our discussions in this book. In Chapter 1 we examine the variety of explanations which have been offered to understand the situation of women in the labour force in Britain in the middle of the twentieth century. Because women's domestic responsibilities had for so long been regarded as 'natural', for decades no explanation of their subordinate position within paid work was seen as necessary. However, feminists such as Hartmann (1982) and Walby (1986) argued that men had systematically excluded women from better jobs for men's own advantage. That is, they argued that masculine exclusionary practices and structures (or 'patriarchy') was responsible for the inferior employment situation of women, as well as the emergence of the *male breadwinner* ideology, in which the man's primary responsibility was seen as being in the area of market work (employment), whilst women take responsibility for domestic work. Chapter 1 also considers contrary arguments. It has been suggested that rather than patriarchal structures and processes excluding women, the structure of women's employment is largely an outcome of the *choices* that women make. This view has recently been restated with some force by Hakim (1996). We also discuss recent developments in feminist theories, which have moved away from a primary emphasis upon the 'equality agenda'—that is, achieving equality of treatment and status between men and women—and towards more of an emphasis upon the question of *difference*, both within the category of 'woman' and men and women, as well as the way in which varying masculinities and femininities are discursively produced and constructed.

In Chapter 2, however, we temporarily suspend our discussion of these theoretical issues in order to examine in more depth the nature and extent of women's employment in Britain. As well as discussing general trends, we also examine two areas of 'non-standard' (that is, not permanent, full-time, 'male breadwinner') employment in which women predominate. These are part-time work, and homeworking. And we examine, too, the phenomenon of *occupational segregation*, that is, the concentration of men into 'men's jobs', and the concentration of women into 'women's jobs'. Here, there is some evidence that women are gaining entry into higher-level occupations. However, overall we find that much of the expansion of women's employment has been in the area of 'non-standard' jobs, and that women's continuing family responsibilities loom large as a reason for taking up and continuing in this kind of paid work. We suggest that, given that women continue to earn considerably less than men, then the lack of state-facilitated and/or subsidised caring in Britain is likely to be a major *structural* factor contributing to women's concentration in non-standard employment, which is indeed flexible, but tends to be poorly paid and lacking in employment-related benefits.

In Chapter 3 we continue with our emphasis upon the importance of structural (contextual) factors in the shaping of women's employment patterns through a cross-national comparison of the structure of women's employment in four countries: Britain, France, Norway, and the Czech Republic. This chapter also includes a comparative examination of a major post-war institution which has shaped women's lives, *the welfare state*. The welfare state has, to varying degrees, assumed some of the caring functions which had been considered women's 'natural' preserve; and it is not surprising, therefore, that different welfare-state 'regimes' (Esping-Andersen 1990) should have had a differential impact upon the structuring of women's employment patterns. However, we also highlight the impact of other aspects of state policy—in particular, the state's approach to mothers and children, and to the question of equality for women more generally—on women's employment.

Our discussion, however, has emphasized the essential *interdependence* of different kinds of 'work': that is, paid work and domestic and/or non-marketed 'work'. In Chapter 4, therefore, we examine the interface between employment and the family. The rise in women's employment has been accompanied by a number of other social trends, including a falling birthrate, a rise in single-parent households, and an increase in the divorce rate. However, has it been accompanied by any change in the domestic division of labour itself? We find that although men are, in general, taking on more hours of domestic work, the rate of change is very slow and, relatively speaking, has run behind that of the increase in the hours of women's paid work. Gershuny *et al.* (1994) describe this process as one of *lagged adaptation*, in which the division of domestic labour is only slowly being adjusted to the realities of women's employment. In particular, it would seem that substantial changes occur only when the woman is in full-time employment. This finding is reinforced by studies of the control of finance within households. Again, it would seem that this control is more egalitarian to the extent that the woman works full-time. That is, the greater the extent of the material resources a woman brings into the household, the more likely she is to exercise power and decision-making within it.

In Chapter 5 we return to the topic of women as employees, and review the sociological history of the study of women and employment from the 1940s and 50s to the present day. Banking, a sector which has been in the process of feminization since the Second World War, is used as a point of reference throughout this chapter. In this industry, women were initially (in the 1960s and 1970s) used as a short-term, flexible labour force only, reflecting and reproducing the pervasiveness of male-breadwinner assumptions about the division of labour between the sexes. However, as both conditions within the industry and the situation of women have changed, so has the banks' utilization of female labour. Women still predominate at the lower levels of the industry, but increasingly they are also moving into managerial positions, reflecting the erosion of vertical occupational segregation that was discussed in Chapter 2. However, these changes do not mean that discrimination against women in employment is a thing of the past. Besides the structural factors considered in Chapters 2 and 3, which are grounded in the assumption that women will take the main responsibility for domestic work and the household, women are still (in some cases) also directly discriminated against within the workplace, as our discussion of sexual harassment demonstrates.

In terms of the 'equality agenda', therefore, there are not many grounds for complacency. However, a number of recent empirical studies of women in employment have emphasized not so much the agenda of equal opportunities, but rather the way in which different masculinities are changed and developed within the world of paid work itself. Organizations (and not just occupations) are seen as 'gendered', drawing upon different *discourses* of masculinity and femininity in the carrying out of particular work roles. These studies reflect the recent developments in feminist theory which were discussed in Chapter 1. However, it is argued that, although the emphasis upon masculine and feminine 'difference' may help us to better understand the workings of organizations and workplaces, as well as circumstances of apparent contradiction, these analyses cannot remove or obliterate the necessity of a focus upon the constraints of 'lived experience' itself if we wish to understand the division of labour between men and women.

In the final chapter, Chapter 6, therefore, we draw together both our emphasis upon the need to understand the gender division of labour as an outcome of constraint and choice, and cultural and psychological perceptions of masculinity and femininity, through Glucksmann's (1995) descriptive concept of the *Total Organization of Social Labour* (TOSL). This describes how the totality of labour in any society is divided up between different institutions and activities. The male-breadwinner model represented one such TOSL, in which 'market' and 'non-market' work was (on the whole) portioned out between the sexes. The male-breadwinner model is being eroded, but what is replacing it? More women are in paid employment, but are employed in a marketized, individualized society in which two jobs are increasingly necessary to support a household. However, households and families are increasingly fragile. Given these trends, material and social polarization is increasing in British society. It is argued that the resolution of this contradiction is not to return to the male-breadwinner model, but rather, to create 'good', well-regulated jobs for both women *and* men. Masculine exclusionary (or patriarchal) practices are extremely resilient (although it has recently been suggested that it is men, rather than women, who lost out within the male-breadwinner TOSL). Nevertheless, we can conclude that, on balance, the gender division of labour between the sexes is becoming increasingly blurred, and with more egalitarian outcomes.

Chapter One

Explaining 'Women's Work'

The Historical Division of Labour

Women and men have always worked together to reproduce social life on a long-term as well as a day-to-day basis. The way in which this 'work' is divided between them, however, has changed and developed over time and still varies considerably between different societies. However, for a number of reasons, most societies have allocated particular tasks to men and others to women—that is, men and women have not usually performed the same work. This gender division of labour has run in parallel with another universal historical fact, which is that men have occupied the dominant positions in society. Primogeniture (inheritance by the eldest son) meant that men were usually the rulers in traditional society, and in contemporary society men hold most of the leading positions in politics and have the best jobs.

Because the gender division of labour has been universal, for many years social scientists had a tendency to regard it as somehow 'natural', that is, as one reflection of biological differences between the sexes. This was reflected in the discussions of the 'founding fathers' of sociology (Stacey 1981). Successive social changes, however, have had a substantial impact on the work of both men and women. For the purposes of our discussion, the historical change of most importance has been the coming of industrial capitalism, or the transition from traditional to 'modern' society.

Before the social and technical changes associated with the Industrial Revolution in the mid-eighteenth century, most production, for both day-to-day use and the market, was to be found in the household or domestic sphere (Bradley 1989). In the seventeenth and early eighteenth centuries the population of England, the 'first industrial nation', was still largely engaged in agricultural work (Laslett 1983). In such households, men, women, and children co-operated in the production of food and basic commodities. Tasks were divided along gender lines;

women cared for poultry and pigs, household tasks, dairying, and other ancillary work such as spinning and sewing, whereas men were responsible for larger animals (horses and cattle), ploughing, and mowing, although in periods of work-intensity such as the harvest both sexes might do similar work.

Many rural households did not have access to sufficient land of their own, or common land, to support a family. Members of the rural poor worked (and very often lived) in other households as servants or labourers; and, in general, the poorer the household the smaller the number of people in it. Artisanal manufacturing—of shoes, metalwork, cloth, and so on—was similarly carried out by household members of all ages and both sexes; and everybody, beyond a very young age, 'worked'. People needed to live and work together in order to survive, and the single-person household was a rarity. The phrase 'household-work strategy' (Pahl 1984) has been used to describe the way in which households not only co-operated in the work to be done, but also gained or lost members, took in homework (such as straw plaiting or laundry), or took on outside (paid) work, in order to survive.

However, household-work strategies, and thus the gender division of labour, were profoundly reshaped with the coming of industrialism. With the development of factory production the population increasingly moved to the expanding towns, and took up wage work rather than household production (although agriculture still remained a major employer of labour, and until after the First World War more women worked in domestic service than in any other occupation). Men became increasingly identified with paid or market work, and women with the household; that is, with non-market work. In contemporary language, the rate of economic activity (that is, paid work) amongst women, particularly married women, declined, and by 1911 only 9.6 per cent of married women were in paid employment (Halsey 1988: 172).

The growing exclusion of married women from paid work was also associated with a shift in the ideology of womanhood. Increasingly, 'good' women became defined as refined and delicate beings, who should best be shielded from the crudities and excesses of the 'public' sphere—which included the world of paid employment (Davidoff and Hall 1987). Women became the 'angel of the house', and the home itself was increasingly defined as a purifying haven, maintained as such by the efforts of its resident spirit (the wife). These ideas, not surprisingly, emerged first of all amongst the bourgeoisie and upper classes who could afford to maintain a non-working wife. However, social reformers, concerned with matters such as infant mortality and the health of

7

the working classes, as well as moral issues such as illegitimacy and prostitution, also considered that these social problems were exacerbated by an absence of domestic comforts, cleanliness, and moral order resulting from women's paid employment. Women, they argued, had domestic responsibilities, particularly those associated with the care of children and other family members, which should take precedence over market work.

Thus the *de facto* exclusion of women from market work was accompanied by the development of the ideology of 'separate spheres', in which the home and domestic sphere was defined as that as belonging to women, whilst that of the outside world—including the workplace— was defined as that of men (Smith 1973). As we have seen, by the beginning of this century there had emerged the male-breadwinner model of the gender division of labour, in which men were held to be largely responsible for market work, whilst women were responsible for domestic work. The male-breadwinner model was explicit in the policies of the Trade Union movement from the nineteenth century onwards, which fought for the principle of the 'family wage'—that is, a wage sufficient for a man to be able to support a wife and family. This close identification of women with the family meant that 'the family' was seen as *the* major causal factor in understanding women's labour market position and behaviour.

Clearly, the fact that women have assumed the major responsibility for household tasks has had a major impact on their participation in market work. The fact that many people saw (and still see) this responsibility as being somehow 'natural' is probably one reason why family-related explanations of women's labour market behaviour have been very influential (see, for example, Hakim's work which is discussed below). However, some feminists have always argued that the key to understanding women's labour-market position lay not in their 'naturally' ordained family responsibilities, but rather in the fact that within the workplace and labour market men had systematically excluded women from better-paying work, and had done this in their own interests (Cockburn 1983). With the advent of 'second-wave' feminism from the 1960s, these kinds of arguments increased in their intensity, and have had a considerable impact within sociology.

'Second-wave' feminism is a term used to describe the feminism which developed in Western countries from the 1960s onwards. The term draws a contrast with 'first-wave' feminism, which developed from the second half of the nineteenth century. 'First-wave' feminism was particularly concerned with gaining women's rights to vote, and other civil equalities with men (such as, for example, property rights for wives, which are discussed in Chapter 4). It was not as concerned with equality for women in the sphere of paid employment, which became a major objective of 'second-wave' feminism. The concept of patriarchy also became very important in 'second-wave' feminist debates.

Patriarchy and Work

Whether the shift of market production from the household to the office and factory made the general position of women better or worse with the coming of industrialism is a matter of debate. Early twentieth-century feminists such as Alice Clark (1982; see also Pinchbeck 1981) argued that the loss of economic activity on the part of married women led to a decline in their status and economic power, forcing them into dependence on men. Their exclusion from productive activity, it was argued, led to a loss of skills as well as of access to positions in artisanal manufacture and trade. Other historians, however, have argued that the coming of industrialism was beneficial as far as the status of women was concerned. Shorter (1976), for example, argues that the position of women in traditional peasant societies was one of complete subordination to men within the household, and that the household also served to confine women. The possibility of waged work for women not only took them out of the household, but also improved their economic position *vis-à-vis* that of their menfolk, in that they could earn money as independent persons.

Although their interpretations differ, both Clark and Shorter take a *materialist* view of history (arguing, that is, that material or economic power and resources ultimately determine social relationships). This perspective is echoed in Engels' (1940) analysis of the 'woman problem' in contemporary capitalism. Women, he argued, would only achieve their liberation from the family if they could achieve economic independence from men—and in an industrial society, this meant waged work. Thus under state socialism, for example, Stalin declared that the 'woman problem' had been solved once married women had been brought into the wage economy, even though in respect of both paid employment and household work the circumstances of women in state socialism were not equal to those of men (Buckley 1989).

Patriarchy means 'the rule of the father', and in the household economy, the father ruled over the household—which, amongst better-off persons and the landowning classes, could include many dozens of people. Thus traditional patriarchs ruled other, subordinate men, as well as women and children. The passing of traditional society not only undermined the power of the patriarch, but also that of other sources of traditional authority such as religion and hereditary rulers. Many traditional or customary rights involved the subordination of other people. However, from the eighteenth century onwards, rights of *individual* freedom were increasingly held to be the most important. Major events such as the French Revolution (1789) and the American War of Independence (1776) were the political manifestations of this movement towards 'modernity', which was also associated with an emphasis upon the 'natural' equality of human beings (Dahrendorf 1969). Nevertheless, the subordination of women persisted and, in current usage, patriarchy has become used as a term to describe the domination of women by men:

I define patriarchy as a set of social relations which has a material base and in which there are hierarchical relations between men, and solidarity among them, which enable them to control women. (Hartmann 1982: 447)

I shall define patriarchy as a system of social structures in which men dominate, oppress, and exploit women. (Walby 1990: 20)

Feminist authors such as Hartmann and Walby have argued that the reshaping of the gender division of labour following on from the development of capitalism was crucial in ensuring the perpetuation of patriarchy. The expansion of wage labour offered the possibility of economic independence for women—as, indeed, was suggested by Shorter. This possibility of the erosion of male power, Hartmann argues, was avoided by ensuring that women were excluded from the better jobs in the wage economy, and were underpaid for the wage work they did do. Thus the gender division of labour in the traditional household economy was reconstituted in the market for wage labour. In traditional patriarchal societies, Hartmann argues, men had already acquired the skills of organization and command, and these were transferred into the wage economy. As a consequence, men now do the same jobs as other men (skilled manual work, management and the professions, particular occupations such as printing and engineering), whilst women do the same jobs as other women (light industrial work, caring occupations, low-level office work). This division of the labour market into 'men's jobs' and 'women's jobs' is a phenomenon known as *occupational segregation*, and its rationale has been described by Hartmann as follows:

Job segregation by sex . . . is the primary mechanism in capitalist society that maintains the superiority of men over women, because it enforces lower wages

Table 1.1 Wage rates in pin-making, 1830s

		per day
Drawing wire	Man	3s. 3d.
Straightening wire	Woman	1s. 0d.
	Girl	0s. 6d.
Pointing	Man	5s. 3d.
Twisting and cutting heads	Boy	0s. 4½d.
	Man	5s. 4½d.
Heading	Woman	1s. 3d.
Tinning or whitening	Man	6s. 0d.
	Woman	3s. 0d.
Papering	Woman	1s. 6d.

Source: Babbage (1832), cited in Braverman (1974: 80)

for women in the labour market. Low wages keep women dependent on men because they encourage women to marry. Married women must perform domestic chores for their husbands. Men benefit, then, from both higher wages and the domestic division of labour. This domestic division of labour, in turn, acts to weaken women's position in the labour market. Thus, the hierarchical domestic division of labour is perpetuated by the labour market, and vice versa. (1982: 448)

The economic consequences of occupational segregation by sex in the nineteenth century are neatly illustrated in Babbage's table of wage rates in pin-making.

All of the men's jobs in pin-making are paid at a higher rate than the women's jobs, and even when women carry out the same task as men, they are paid at half of the men's rate.

In the British case, Walby (1986) has argued that patriarchal occupational segregation has been achieved by a combination of two strategies. First, women have been directly excluded from a wide range of occupations—from apprenticeships and trade-union membership (once essential to get a job) in skilled crafts and industries such as engineering and printing, as well as from practically the whole range of professional occupations from medicine to the arts (such as architecture), finance professions, and the law. Second, women have been confined to jobs which are graded lower than those of men (for example, becoming nurses rather than doctors). This latter strategy has been particularly prevalent in expanding 'white-collar' occupations such as clerical work—where, indeed, lower-paid 'women-only' grades persisted until the 1960s in industries such as banking. Exclusion strategies, Walby argues, dominated in the nineteenth century, segregation strategies in the twentieth.

Trade unions, which have been organized largely by men on behalf of men, have played the major role in developing the strategies of exclusion and grading with segregation in the workplace. However, they have not been the only source of patriarchal intervention, and Walby argues that government policies have been particularly important. During the nineteenth century the Factory Acts, which restricted the extent of women's employment (particularly in the cotton industry), were an important way in which the state acted in the maintenance of patriarchal interests. Another example of the state's role in supporting patriarchy, Walby argues, relates to the use of women's labour during the two world wars. With the agreement of the trade unions, women were recruited into jobs (particularly in engineering but also in 'white-collar' occupations such as finance) which had previously been reserved for men. After the war women were, sometimes unwillingly, removed from these occupations and returned to their 'proper' sphere—that of domesticity. Male workers and the state, together, particularly in the nineteenth century, with bourgeois philanthropists who wished to impose their own morality on working-class family life, thus preserved the access for men in general to women's unpaid labour within the household.

These kinds of policies, however, deprived employers of access to women's (cheaper) labour (indeed, the nineteenth-century Factory Acts were often opposed by the employers). A compromise therefore had to be made between the rather different requirements of employers (who wanted cheap and docile labour) and domestic patriarchs (husbands who wanted women's work within the home). After the Second World War Walby argues that this was achieved through the development of part-time work for married women, which gave employers access to women's cheaper labour whilst preserving the domestic division of labour within the household. Thus, in 1986 Walby concluded:

I dispute the theories of those who argue that it is women's position in the family which leads them to choose a lesser form of engagement in paid work than men. Rather the issue is, why do women suffer such appalling conditions of work in the family as many do? Why do most women marry on such terms? The answer is that the options for most women in paid work are not much better, because men have usually been successful in excluding women from the better forms of work. (248)

Both Hartmann and Walby, therefore, have argued that, historically, occupational segregation is largely a consequence of deliberate patriarchal strategies undertaken by men in order to secure the best jobs (best in the sense both of best-paid as well as being closest to the structures of power and domination in society) as well as maintaining their access to the domestic labour of women. Walby's work, in particular, might be seen as arguing that within the male-breadwinner model of the family, women are definitely the losers.

Other feminists have developed a somewhat different historical account. Humphries (1982), for example, argued that the persistence of the working-class family was itself a reflection of the working-class struggle against the power of capitalist employers and the negative impact of the spread of wage labour and individualized market relations. Traditional society might have bound and subordinated the individual as such, but the traditional lord or patriarch also had an obligation to support his less-fortunate dependents in times of hardship. 'The market' has no such customary obligations; and without some kind of protection individuals who have no property, or have nothing to offer that the market will buy (that is, they are unemployed), or are vulnerable through age or sickness, risk total destitution. During the early decades of capitalist development, Humphries argues, the working-class family was a source of social support, and kin relationships had a material base, providing material support in times of unemployment, illness, or other crises. Kin networks provided access to jobs, and following the Poor Law of 1834 families struggled to keep their members out of the workhouse, which was dreaded precisely because whilst providing the means of life (that is, food and clothing) it also split up families. 'Kinship ties,' Humphries argued, 'were strengthened because they provided the only framework controllable by the working class, within which reciprocation could occur that was sufficiently defined to provide an adequate guarantee of assistance in crisis situations' (1982: 481).

Humphries also argues that the exclusion of women from paid work should not be seen one-sidedly, as being primarily a mechanism used by men for the oppression of women. Preventing women's employment in particular jobs, she argues, was an important aspect of the working-class struggle to control the *supply* of labour (that is, people available for jobs) and thus its price. If fewer members of the working class were available for employment, then employers could not drive down wages even further. Humphries' (1984) analysis of the debates around the passing of the 1842 Mines Act, which prevented women and children from working underground, also questions whether women's exclusion from paid work can, in fact, be regarded as an example of the state's collusion with working men in the subordination of women. As we have seen above, this has been argued by Walby in respect of the Factory Acts. Humphries points out that the sexual division of labour in the mines meant that men were not in competition with women for the same kind of work—men hewed the coal, women and children were engaged in transport and processing. Work teams were usually family teams, and colliers who were forced to use non-family labour were faced with extra expenses. Men did not stand to gain, therefore, from the exclusion of women and children from underground working, although on the whole they supported the ban on underground work. Furthermore, there was no evidence that the colliers wished to achieve a greater level of home comforts through an increase in their wives' domestic labour. Rather, Humphries argues that the major ideological force pressing to remove women from the pits and into the domestic sphere were the (male) bourgeois moralizers and reformers, who were horrified by the extent of female nakedness in the pit (in close proximity to male workers), and its possible implications for loose (that is, sexual) behaviour.

In her analyses, Humphries is arguing that the family, rather than the individual (male) worker, was deeply implicated in production even at a time when the 'separation of home and work' was supposedly taking place. Economics, she argues (and Humphries was writing as a Marxist-feminist economist) has systematically ignored the significance of the family; it is treated as if it were a 'black box', and what goes on in it is seen as irrelevant to economic analysis. This, she argues, is a misleading assumption. Similarly, she suggests that feminists such as Hartmann and Walby have assumed, rather than demonstrated, that men gained direct benefits from the exclusion of women. She does, however, agree that although the working class as a whole may have benefited from the gradual institution of the principle of the 'family wage', women, relatively, lost out—that is, it cannot be assumed that class interests and women's interests are the same.[1]

Whether the gender division of labour in employment should be seen largely as an outcome of patriarchal exclusion ('patriarchy first' arguments), or class struggle and the development of capitalism ('capitalism first' arguments), is not an issue that will be pursued here. Rather, the view will be developed in this book that explanations of the structuring of the gender division of labour will prove to be multi-stranded, and that single-factor explanations should be avoided. The debates around the exclusion of married women from the labour force, however, do serve to highlight a point which will be developed and emphasized in this book—that is, the essential interdependence of family (domestic) work-patterns and market work-patterns. As we have seen, the coming of modern industrialism is widely understood as having led to the *separation* of the home and workplace, and this was described in the ideology of 'separate spheres'. However, although home and work might have been *physically* separated, what went on in the workplace was crucially dependent on what went on in the home, and vice versa.

For example, the full-time, long-term, male-breadwinner model of 'standard employment' depended crucially upon the presence of a domestic worker/carer, particularly if there were children (Beck 1992). Glucksmann (1995) describes this interdependence of domestic work and market work as constituting the 'Total Social Organization of Labour', or TSOL for short. The TSOL is simply a description of how the totality of labour in any particular society is divided up between different institutions and activities. For example, a society in which most of the manual work was done by slaves, such as in ancient Rome, would have a very different TOSL to early-twentieth-century Britain.

Recognizing that wage work and domestic work are interdependent raises the question of what we actually mean by the term 'work'. We may want to see necessary caring or housework as 'work', but for the purposes of sociological analysis, we have to be able to distinguish between what is 'work' and what is not, otherwise the term becomes meaningless. The same activity may or may not be 'work' depending upon both place and the set of relationships in which the activity is embedded. Glucksmann uses and extends Pahl's (1988) example of a woman ironing a shirt. Such a woman may be working in a laundry, ironing for pay, or ironing for someone else (or in someone else's home) for the same reason. A woman may be ironing for her family, that is, carrying out unpaid domestic work. Or a woman might be ironing a shirt for a lover, as an expression of her attachment and devotion. Is this 'work'? Pahl suggests that it is not, but is rather more a symbolic expression of emotion, an expression of interpersonal relationships. To these examples of ironing, Glucksmann adds a further instance: ironing as a forced activity, extracted under the threat of physical violence. Is this 'work'? Glucksmann argues that it is not. Rather, she suggests that 'forced ironing' is better understood as being action carried out under the constraint of *personal* power relations (1995: 70).

We have argued that the gender division of labour has multiple causes. Relations of gender are constructed at different levels of analysis; at the levels of the state and its institutions, in organizations and occupations, in social activities and sport, as well as in the household and interpersonal relations. There is no single 'theory' which can explain this complex 'gendering' of societies at all levels. In this book, therefore, the concept of patriarchy will be used in a largely descriptive, rather than an analytical, fashion (Pollert 1996). Gender relations *may* be patriarchal (in fact, they often are), but they do not *have* to be so. Thus we will be using the term in a general sense to describe situations in which men have organized to exclude and dominate women, but it will not be employed as a complete explanation (or 'theory') of the position of women in society, or of their position in the labour force.

One feature of the 'patriarchy *vs.* capitalism' debate, however, was that despite their disagreements the participants shared a materialist approach which also incorporated the view that gender relations (even if patriarchal), and thus the gender division of labour, are *socially* constructed rather than being biological or 'natural'. That is, both Clark and Shorter, as well as Hartmann, Walby, and Humphries, would share in the view that the gender division of labour does not simply depend upon individual tastes and preferences, or some kind of 'innate' difference between men and women, but rather reflects the historical and social context in which it is developed. This view, however, has recently been challenged.

Individualist Explanations of Women's Work: Hakim

Hakim was one of the first authors to identify and describe the phenomenon of occupational segregation by sex in Britain. In an important paper for the then Department of Employment (1979), she not only identified the contours of occupational segregation, but also described in broad outline the pattern of women's employment in Britain during this century. She demonstrated how, since the Second World War, married women had increasingly entered the paid labour force after their youngest child had reached school age, leading to the emergence of the characteristic 'double peaked' employment profile for British women, that is, a high level of market work in the younger age groups, followed by a fall as women reach childbearing age, followed by another increase from the mid-thirties onwards (Chapter 2 will be describing women's employment patterns in more detail, and we will not pursue this here).

In a series of recent publications, Hakim (1991, 1995, 1996) has addressed herself to the question of explaining the particular structure of women's employment in Britain, and why it differs from that of men.

This would mean explaining patterns of occupational segregation, the prevalence of part-time or 'non-standard' work amongst women, and so on. As we have seen, the authors we have discussed so far have all pointed to the significance of what may be broadly described as materialist or structural factors in shaping women's employment patterns, which include the decline of traditional society and the coming of industrialism, together with the actions of capitalist employers, the state, and organised masculine exclusionary practices. In contrast, however, Hakim argues that individual *tastes and preferences* are more important. She argues that the fact that there are different 'types' of women, with differing levels of 'work commitment', largely explains the structuring of women's employment in contemporary Britain. Hakim argues that there are two 'qualitatively different' types of working woman, the 'committed' and the 'uncommitted', the former giving priority to their employment careers, the latter to their domestic responsibilities. 'Committed' women work full-time, 'uncommitted' women work part-time.

The existence of these two types of women lends support to rational-choice and human-capital theories, argues Hakim. Rational-choice and human-capital theories have been developed by economists in order to explain the pattern of women's work. Becker (1985) is a human-capital theorist who argues that the sexual division of labour in the home—particularly women's role in childbearing and -rearing—leads them to specialize in domestic work and economize in the effort they put into their paid employment; that is, women invest less in their 'human capital'. Conversely, it is rational for men to invest more in their 'human capital', given that there will be no other claims (such as domestic duties) on their efforts. Thus women who are 'uncommitted' in their work (that is, employment) orientations make a rational decision to take up particular kinds of work, such as part-time work and homeworking, as they have chosen to give priority to their domestic lives.

These choices by different types of women, argues Hakim, explain otherwise surprising findings—such as, for example, the fact that part-time workers, who do not enjoy particularly good pay or job security, often say that they are very 'satisfied' with their employment because it allows them to fulfil their domestic priorities (we will be discussing part-time work in Chapter 2). Somewhat contentiously, Hakim has described such women as 'grateful slaves' (1991). In contrast, 'committed' women (who are usually middle-class) give priority to their market work rather than their domestic work and, in line with the prescriptions of human-capital theory, will choose to invest in their employment

careers by gaining qualifications, not having breaks in their employment careers, and so on.

Women, therefore, are divided amongst themselves. Uncommitted
women value domesticity more than work, and are unhappy with other
women who step out of female roles, such as female bosses. Here
Hakim's explanation draws upon Goldberg's sociobiological theory of
male dominance. Goldberg argues that hormonal differences between
men and women make men more 'self-assertive, aggressive, dominant
and competitive'.

In consequence they invariably seek to obtain the top positions in any hierarchy,
such as the top positions in political or other public leadership hierarchies, the
highest status jobs or roles in the workforce . . . or any other area of social activity
with a hierarchy of status and power that prompts competitive behaviour.
(Hakim 1996: 5)

Here individual tastes and preferences are seen as being, in part, *bio-
logically* determined. The fact that women are fundamentally divided
within themselves (between 'committed' and 'uncommitted'), Hakim
argues, serves to amplify the effect of these natural masculine characteristics, and men are, as a consequence, disproportionately successful
in the sphere of employment.

The thrust of Hakim's argument, therefore, is that the nature and
pattern of women's labour-force participation is largely a consequence
of women's choices, and that the heterogeneity of women's employment statuses reflects the heterogeneity of female choice. She is very
critical of feminists such as Hartmann and Walby, who have argued that
occupational segregation has been an important mechanism whereby
women have been deliberately denied access to jobs which would allow
them to live independently. In contrast, Hakim argues that:

Occupational segregation has been reconstructed in the late twentieth century
to provide separate occupations and jobs for women following the marriage
career, which allows only non-committed contingent work and non-career jobs
which are always subordinate to non-market activities . . . it . . . makes sense of
the contemporary features of female dominated occupations, with the highest
incidence of part-time work, the lowest incidence of unsocial hours, the lowest
levels of trade union membership and the ability to tolerate high turnover levels.
(1995: 450)

It may be noted that this explanation does not address the problem of
disparities in power and resources between men and women in the
labour market. Rather, the status quo is being described as a reflection
of the requirements of a population differentiated by variations in individual 'choice' alone, rather than by any other differences in material

resources, opportunities, constraints on behaviour, and so on. As far as men and women are concerned, it would be difficult to argue that this has been or is the case. The structural constraints on women's capacities to operate in the labour market, and in particular occupations, have been extensively documented (Cockburn 1991; Crompton and Jones 1984). It is not being argued here that individual women do not have choices and preferences. They do, and labour-market outcomes must be regarded as being shaped by both choice *and* constraint (Crompton and Sanderson 1990). To restate the major principle that informs this book, the gender division of labour is the outcome of a number of factors, and 'choice' is one of them.

Hakim is generally critical of feminist commentators on women's employment. She claims they have had a tendency to treat women as if they were a homogeneous, undifferentiated category who all want to work full-time on the same terms as men. Furthermore, she argues, these feminists have described women's employment situation as if it were completely determined by structural constraints, that is, 'external' factors: 'theory and research on women's employment seems particularly prone to an over-socialised view of women, or with structural factors so heavily weighted that choice flies out of the window' (1991: 114). It may be suggested that in developing her own explanation, Hakim goes too far in the other direction, in that women's employment patterns are being explained in almost wholly voluntarist, individualistic terms. The point must also be made that 'feminists' are not a homogeneous category either. It is true that authors such as Hartmann and Walby have emphasized the significance of legislation, institutional structures, and organized male activity such as trade-union strategies in shaping women's employment patterns; but there are other strands within feminism which have given equal emphasis to the importance of individual and interpersonal factors.

'Difference' Feminism, Feminist Theory, and the Analysis of Women's Employment

Feminist politics has always been characterized by a tension between 'equality' and 'difference'. One way of illustrating this is through the example of debates over protective legislation for women in employment. 'Difference' feminists (more often described as 'welfare' feminists in this context) have historically argued that, because of women's capacity to bear (and usually rear) children, as well as other physical differences from men in strength, ability to endure harsh conditions, and so on, protective legislation for women in employment is necessary. In contrast, 'equality' feminists have argued that any special treatment required for women as women—such as working shorter hours—will make them less attractive to employers and have the effect of disadvantaging them in the competition with men for employment (Banks 1981). These kinds of debates about practicalities have been reflected in theoretical debates within feminism. It has been argued that women's psychological development is 'different' from that of men. Chodorow (1978; 1989), for example, has argued that small boys have to make a break from their primary carer—their mother—in order to achieve their masculinity and thus their independent being, whereas girls do not have to undergo this distancing. In consequence, women are more nurturing and have a greater capacity for 'connectedness' than men, and this is reflected in their work as well as in their interpersonal relationships.

Are men and women, therefore, *essentially* 'different' from each other? Given the differences in their early socialization, and parental treatment, as well as hormonal and other physical and biological differences, it would be amazing if women in aggregate did not differ from men in aggregate. Women and men *are* different, but the argument that these 'differences' correspond to some kind of essential 'masculinity' or 'femininity' is problematic. This is because of the second aspect of 'difference' which has been debated by feminists: the difference both within masculinities and femininities and between different categories of women (in class, ethnicity, age, sexual orientation, and so on) (Barrett 1987). Ideas of masculinity and femininity change over time and place: compare, for example, today's fashion for extreme thinness in women with the voluptuous curves of Edwardian beauties. Sensitive and caring 'new men' are still viewed as highly masculine, even though they are very different from the unemotional, physically tough 'macho man' model which arguably prevailed until the 1960s (and is, of course, still in being). Connell (1995) has also described the generation and evolution of different types of gay masculinity.

Recent debates in feminism have been much taken up with these questions. As far as the area of employment is concerned, there would seem to be an emerging consensus amongst researchers informed by a feminist perspective that it is necessary to work simultaneously within the frameworks of 'equality' and 'difference':

Men tell us 'women cannot claim to be equal if they are different from men. You have to choose.' We now have a reply. . . . as women, we can be both the same as you *and* different from you . . . We can also be both the same and different from each other. What we are seeking is not in fact *equality*, but *equivalence*, not *sameness* for individual women and men, but *parity* for women as a sex. (Cockburn 1991: 10–11)

Feminist thinking has been influenced by a wide variety of theories in social science.[2] Both Hartmann and Walby's work was much influenced by the rediscovery of Marx (or neo-Marxism) in the 1960s and 1970s, and this is reflected in their materialist emphases. In recent years post-modernism, post-structuralism, and psychoanalytic theory have all been influential in feminist debates. Post-modernist theories empha-size the rapidly changing and surface nature of the modern world. They argue that important theoretical ideas associated with the development of modernity—such as, for example, the belief in the rational basis of individual freedom and liberation (and, as we have seen, these ideas were very important in the erosion of traditional patriarchal systems) can no longer be believed. Lyotard (1984), for example, argues that they are 'myths'. Lyotard argues that the 'myth of liberation' has been under-mined by the way in which science has contributed to twentieth-century crimes such as the Holocaust, and the creation of weapons of mass destruction. The 'myth of truth' (the idea that absolute explana-tions can be identified) has also been taken over by *relativism*. Relativ-ism is an intellectual position which rejects universal or absolute standards or criteria—for example of morality, or personal behaviour. The influence of relativism can be seen in the emphasis upon 'differ-ence' within recent feminist theories, which have argued that there can be no absolute (or single) category of 'woman'.

Post-structuralism is the same as post-modernism in its relativism. This approach also de-emphasizes the significance of formal, seem-ingly concrete institutional structures (such as formal bureaucracies, and/or other rules and regulations, even material conditions) in the explanation and understanding of behaviour. Post-structuralism em-phasizes the importance of language in the structuring of the social sphere, but the language it emphasizes is that actually used by people, rather than codified as formal grammar and text. The idea of discourse (often associated with the work of the French theorist Foucault) is very important here. The notion of discourse relates to the chains of mean-ings and concepts—Foucault called them 'discursive formations'—which actually go to 'make up' a social object. Thus different discourses of masculinity and femininity may be identified, for example, as we have already seen in the case of 'new man' versus 'macho man'. Gender itself, that is, masculinities and femininities, are seen not as fixed enti-ties, but as constructed in social interaction.

Thus feminist researchers have explored the way in which different femininities are drawn upon and developed within the workplace (that is, draw upon different discourses of femininity). In her study of secretaries, Pringle (1988) explores how the construction of different sexualities, as well as family relations (submissive femininity, assertive feminist, mother-son, mother-daughter, and so on) enter into the range of different possible relationships amongst the supervisor and the supervised. She states:

Rather than taking 'woman' or 'secretary' as unitary categories I look at the way in which they are constructed. This involves a consideration of the unconscious processes, the repressions and the fantasies that structure 'consciousness', of the precariousness of 'identity' and of the ways in which 'experience' is interpreted through existing discourses. (p. x)

(Note that in this extract, Pringle is also rejecting the notion that there is a universal category of 'woman'). Other ethnographic and case-study research on working (employed) women has similarly described the way in which women in the workplace are not only constituted as 'different' from men, but are also sorted into different categories of woman (Purcell 1988). Women's maternal identification can be particularly important here—for example, a study of school-meals workers ('dinner ladies'), all mothers themselves, demonstrated how they had been able to endure, and ultimately rationalize, worsening conditions of employment 'for the sake of the children' (Crompton and Sanderson 1990).

These recent theoretical developments are complex and often difficult to follow, and this is not a book of feminist theory (however, a rather more critical stance *vis-à-vis* recent feminist theorizing will be developed in Chapters 5 and 6). However, it is not contentious or difficult to note that developments in theory will have an effect upon the nature of the issues studied, and the way in which they are approached, and the study of women and work is no exception. For the moment, however, we will simply note that, contrary to Hakim's assertions, feminists who have studied women's employment have been sensitive to the differences not only between men and women, but also between different groups of women.

Summary and Conclusions

In this chapter, it has been suggested that two major categories of explanation for the division of market work between men and women may be identified:

Emphasis upon social and economic structuring

- Capitalist development and class struggle.
- The development of 'separate spheres' ideology and the activities of bourgeois reformers.
- Patriarchal organization and exclusion.

Emphasis upon individualist explanations

- Human capital theory.
- Psychological (biological) differences between men and women.
- Differences in individual women's work orientations.

These varying explanations have often been debated as if they were either/or alternatives, as if *either* 'patriarchy' *or* capitalism had to be given priority in explaining the position of women in the labour market with the coming of industrialism, as if *either* structural constraints, *or* individual choice, would give us the answer if we want to understand women's contemporary location in the structure of employment.

However, another point which has been stressed in this chapter is an emphasis upon the multi-strandedness of any explanation of gender relations, the gender division of labour, and 'women's work'. We should therefore anticipate that both capitalism and patriarchal processes, structural factors and individual choices, rather than any single theory of 'patriarchy', will contribute to an explanation of the complex totality of women's employment.

Our discussions have also led us to another conclusion relating to the nature of 'work' in contemporary societies, which is of particular importance to our understanding of the structuring of women's work and which cannot be over-emphasised. This is the continuing interdependence of household/domestic work and market work, even in a 'market' society.

Today, the labour market usually hires individuals, rather than families, and the market is usually thought of as actively promoting and leading to an increased individualism. Collectivism, including oligopolies and trade unions, are seen as working 'against' the 'free' or 'self-regulating' market. However, as Humphries and others have argued (see in particular Polanyi 1957), individuals need some kind of protection against an unregulated market, otherwise the weakest will simply be left to starve. Families have often assumed this role (as well as other, more formal institutions, such as the welfare state and mutual support organizations such as trade unions and friendly societies).

Families are supposed to operate on principles of love and affection and to satisfy emotional needs, rather than the principles of rational calculation, pursuit of advantage, and the satisfaction of material needs, such as are found in the market. Family principles and market principles are in tension with each other; indeed, today it is often argued that the pursuit of individual gratification and satisfaction will undermine the family, as reflected, for example, in rising divorce rates. Nevertheless, rather as household work and market work are intertwined, so may psychological and emotional needs—such as the construction of masculinities and femininities—be met in the workplace as well as in the market, as authors like Pringle have suggested.

All of these issues, and their consequences for women's work, will be explored in the following chapters. In the first place, however, we will be examining the structure of paid employment amongst women in Britain today.

LIVERPOOL
JOHN MOORES UNIVERSITY
AVRIL ROBARTS LRC
TITHEBARN STREET
LIVERPOOL L2 2ER
TEL. 0151 231 4022

Chapter Two

The Structure of Women's Employment in Britain Today

Introduction: Historical Trends

Over the last six decades, women's employment has been steadily rising. Figure 2.1 describes the trends in the gender composition of the British labour force over this century. It can be seen that the proportion of the population of working age or more who are 'economically active'—that is, in employment or looking for work—has remained remarkably stable at around 60 per cent or so, more usually above than below this figure (the base for this figure includes people over retirement age, and the proportion of people of working age economically active will be higher). However, the gender composition of the labour force has changed considerably. In the early years of this century, over 90 per cent of all men of working age or more were economically active. This figure did not change much until after the Second World War, but has since declined steadily to only 73 per cent by 1991. Women's employment has moved in the other direction. Up until after the Second World War (1951) only about a third of all women of working age or more were economically active. Since 1951, however, women's employment has been growing steadily, and by 1991 half of all women of working age or more were economically active. Using the same data but describing it in a rather different way, women constituted 29 per cent of the labour force in Britain in 1911, and 29 per cent in 1951, but this had risen to 34 per cent by 1966 and had reached 43 per cent by 1991.

Clearly, there has been a substantial restructuring of the gender division of labour over the last forty years. Its broad outlines may be described in very simple terms. The proportion of men in the labour force has declined, both as a consequence of a rise in the number of years spent in further education and training amongst the younger age groups, and because of an increased rate of (voluntary and involuntary)

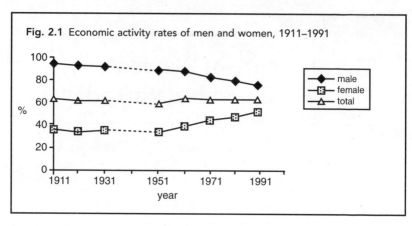

Fig. 2.1 Economic activity rates of men and women, 1911–1991

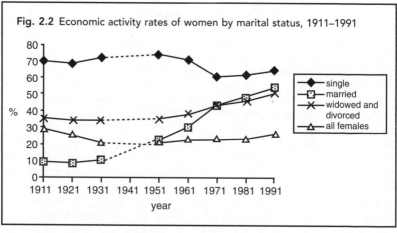

Fig. 2.2 Economic activity rates of women by marital status, 1911–1991

retirement amongst men over fifty. Years spent in further education and training have risen amongst young women as well, but this has been more than counterbalanced by the increase in married women's employment. In Chapter 1, we described in brief the way in which married women were gradually excluded from paid employment after the Industrial Revolution. By the early decades of the twentieth century married women's employment had fallen to just under 10 per cent, and fell even more in the inter-war period. Figure 2.2 describes employment changes for women since 1911, grouped by different marital statuses. Since the 1930s, not only have more women got married but, as this figure demonstrates, more married women have gone out to work; by

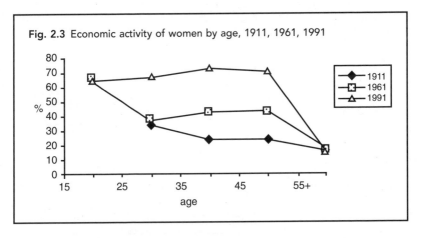

Fig. 2.3 Economic activity of women by age, 1911, 1961, 1991

1991, 53 per cent of married women were in employment or seeking work. In contrast, the variations in participation rates amongst single, and widowed and divorced, women are much less striking.

Age breakdowns illustrate in more detail the trends in women's employment careers over this century. Three years have been selected for comparison: the earliest year for which we have comparable figures, which is 1911; 1961, by which time the increase in married women's employment was well under way; and 1991, the most recent year for which these figures are available. Figures 2.4 and 2.5 give details of women's rates of participation in employment by age for single and married women. First, however, let's look at the picture for all women, in Figure 2.3.

In the early years of this century participation rates amongst young women were around 65 per cent—a very similar figure to today's—but had declined sharply by the 1920s and continued to decline as women got older. By 1961 the pattern had changed. Participation rates among young women were still around their 1911 level, but the decline in economic activity in the 20 year age groups was not as sharp, and economic activity rates began to rise again for women aged 30 and over. The 1961 pattern illustrates the characteristic 'double-peaked' employment profile of British women, which had emerged by the middle of this century. Participation rates amongst young women are relatively high, falling sharply as women enter their childbearing years and stay at home to rear their children, but starting to rise again from the thirties as women return to paid employment, usually after the youngest child has started school. By 1991, however, the picture has

27

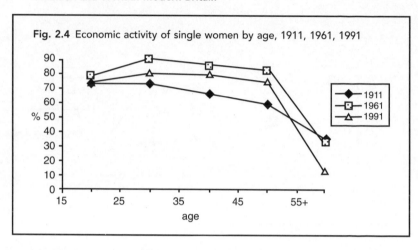

Fig. 2.4 Economic activity of single women by age, 1911, 1961, 1991

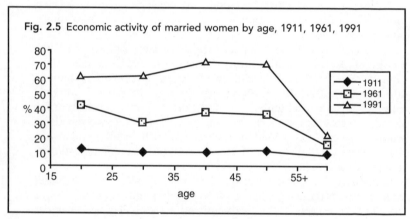

Fig. 2.5 Economic activity of married women by age, 1911, 1961, 1991

changed yet again, and participation rates in the youngest age group are still around 65 per cent, but rise until the 35 to 44 age group.

Giving separate details for single and married women makes the picture clearer, as shown in Figures 2.4 and 2.5.

Figure 2.4 shows that participation rates amongst single women have always been relatively high, but have fallen amongst the youngest age groups—the effect of increasing numbers of young women staying on at school and going into higher education—although they are higher in the older age groups than they were at the beginning of this century.

The changes for married women, however, are much more dramatic (Figure 2.5). In 1911 participation rates were uniformly low at all ages. By 1961, the characteristic double-peaked employment profile is very evident, but the proportion of married women who are economically active is still lower amongst the older age groups. By 1991, however, the proportion of older married women in employment actually exceeds that of the younger, and it is apparent that most women, in or out of partnerships, will 'go out to work' for most of their adult lives.

Our discussion so far, however, has focused only on rates of economic activity. In the broadest of terms, the economic activity rates of men and women would seem to be converging (Figure 2.1). However, these figures tell us nothing about the kind of work that men and women do, and as we shall see, here the differences between the sexes remain very important indeed. Women's working patterns not only vary over the life cycle in comparison to men's, but women's hours of work differ as well. In addition, as we discussed in Chapter 1, men and women are clustered in different jobs—the phenomenon known as occupational segregation. In the rest of this chapter we will discuss these differences in greater detail.

Women and 'Non-Standard' Employment

Full-time work, undertaken without a break from youth until retirement age, is often referred to as 'standard' employment. This was the kind of work which was thought of as providing a 'family wage'; and over the nineteenth and early twentieth centuries the Trade Union movement in Britain struggled to make secure, full-time work available to all adult men—that is, 'male breadwinners'. Feminists have criticized the notion of the 'family wage', pointing out that by no means all women had a 'male breadwinner', and that in any case the breadwinner could not necessarily be relied upon to hand over sufficient to his wife for the material support of the family (as we shall see in Chapter 4, even women who received regular housekeeping money from their husbands often did not know how much he earned). Where women did not have a breadwinner but did have family responsibilities (as in the case of lone parents, or separated, divorced, or deserted women), their exclusion from the better jobs available meant that they had great difficulty in supporting a household (Barrett and Mackintosh 1980).

Not all 'standard' full-time employment, therefore, has necessarily been secure and well-paid. Women have held a disproportionate number of such relatively poor jobs. However, in recent decades, the proportion of permanent full-time jobs has been in decline, and the proportion of 'non-standard' jobs has been rising. 'Non-standard' employment includes part-time work; self-employment; short contract and subcontract work; as well as homeworking, which might fall into any of these categories.

To fully explain the reasons for the increase in non-standard employment over the last twenty years would require a book in itself. There can be little doubt that one major reason for the increase in part-time work is the desire of women to combine paid work with looking after their families. Indeed, much of the part-time work which was generated in the 1950s and 1960s was created by employers to fit in around women's domestic responsibilities. This included the 'twilight shift' in the early evening, when young children could be cared for by the returning 'male breadwinner'. This arrangement enabled women to fulfill their 'two roles'—home and work (that is, employment) (Myrdal and Klein 1956).

However, since the late 1970s the expansion of non-standard employment has taken on further political and economic dimensions. The Conservative government has deliberately deregulated (or 're-regulated') the labour market in order to promote employment flexibility with the aim of improving economic efficiency. Whether or not Britain's economic performance has actually improved as a result is still being debated (we will discuss the social consequences of these trends in Chapters 4 and 6). Another reason why non-standard employment has increased is the expansion of the service sector, including caring services (for example, as provided by children or the elderly) as well as all kinds of leisure and entertainment. Retail hours have increased as well, further increasing the demand for part-time workers in particular. All of these industries and occupations require employment outside standard hours, including weekend work (eds. Crompton *et al.* 1996).

The distribution of non-standard employment is different for men and women. Women predominate amongst part-time workers, although the proportion of male part-timers has been rising. Women are also more likely to be in temporary work than are men (Beatson 1995*a*, *b*). However, self-employment, which is the form of non-standard employment which has grown most rapidly in the recent past (from 7 per cent to 13 per cent between 1979 and 1990), has risen much faster amongst men than women. In 1994 18 per cent of the male workforce in employment was self-employed, the comparable proportion for women being 7 per cent. Self-employment has many different forms—

consider the difference between a retail shop owner or stallholder, an agency nurse, a subcontract worker in the building industry, and a management consultant. The proportion of self-employment amongst women rose from 20 per cent in 1971 to 25 per cent by 1994; but in this chapter we will focus on two of the most 'feminized' types of non-standard work—part-time work, and homeworking.

Part-Time Employment

In Britain, from the 1950s to the 1980s, almost all of the increase in women's employment was in part-time work. In 1951 part-time women workers constituted 12 per cent of the female labour force; this had risen to 22 per cent by 1961 and to 34 per cent by 1971 (Beechey and Perkins 1987). Figure 2.6 shows the growth of part-time work (that is, employees working thirty hours a week or less) since 1971.

Part-time work grew fastest in the early 1970s, and its expansion was actually higher over the period 1971 to 1981 (averaging 3 per cent a year)

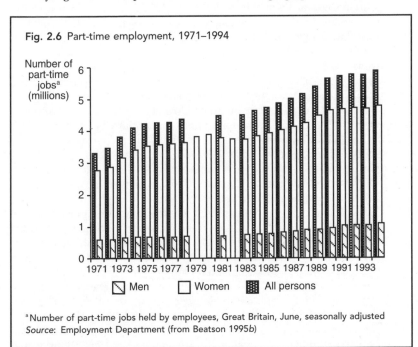

Fig. 2.6 Part-time employment, 1971–1994

Number of part-time jobs[a] (millions)

☒ Men   ☐ Women   ▦ All persons

[a] Number of part-time jobs held by employees, Great Britain, June, seasonally adjusted
Source: Employment Department (from Beatson 1995b)

than it was for the period 1981 to 1994 (2.6 per cent) a year (Beatson 1995*b*: 7). In recent years, part-time work has actually been expanding faster for men than for women; but nevertheless it remains a predominantly female form of employment, and in 1994 78 per cent of part-time jobs were held by women.

Part-time work is also predominantly a form of married women's employment. The Women and Employment survey (Martin and Roberts 1984) showed that, in 1981, 52 per cent of women returning to the labour force after a break for childrearing went back into some kind of part-time employment. Re-entry into part-time employment was also very often associated with occupational downgrading (most commonly women who had had some kind of white-collar job returning to low-level service work). As might have been expected, the age of children affected the number of hours worked, and in general the survey also showed that younger the working woman's youngest child, the shorter the number of hours in employment.

The close association of women with part-time work in Britain has been open to a number of explanations and interpretations. As we have seen in Chapter 1, some feminists, notably Walby, have suggested that the expansion of part-time employment represents a kind of compromise between capitalist employers and domestic patriarchs, in that employers have gained access to women's cheap and docile labour, whilst at the same time leaving them free to carry out domestic labour in the home. This argument has some substance, but is probably more appropriate for some historical periods than others.

During the economic boom that followed the Second World War, the growth of part-time work for women, particularly in manufacturing industry, may be seen as having been largely as a response to the labour shortages which prevailed at that time. As we have seen, women's domestic responsibilities were assumed to be 'natural', and it was therefore assumed, in Britain at any rate, that special working arrangements would have to be made if women were to be brought into the labour force (note that it was not assumed that the state or employers should provide childcare so that women could work longer hours, which might have been another alternative). During this period of labour shortage, part-time work for married women was explicitly seen as a compromise between the employers' demand for labour and women's 'natural' domestic responsibilities. However, from the 1970s, successive economic crises have meant that labour shortages are no more, and unemployment has inexorably risen. During the 1970s and 1980s, the possibility was widely debated as to whether women's employment, which had been expanding in response to the growing demand for labour, would be cut back as demand fell (Beechey and Perkins 1987, Rubery *et al.* 1988). In fact, as we have seen in Figure 2.6, women's part-time work carried on growing during this period.

The 1980s were also a period of economic restructuring and massive deindustrialization in Britain, and jobs in industry have disappeared at an incredible rate. In 1971, 36.4 per cent of jobs were in manufacturing and 52.6 per cent in services, whereas by 1993, 72.8 per cent of jobs were in services and 20.4 per cent in manufacturing. Thus it may be suggested that, over the last few decades, the major post-war advantage of part-time work to employers—as a way of supplementing the labour supply by drawing married women into the labour market—has shifted. Today, part-time work is considered advantageous mainly because of its *flexibility*. Indeed, the significance of part-time workers in the ← flexible labour force has been very much emphasized in a recent review which is also very positive about employee flexibility in general (Beatson 1995*a*, *b*). It must also be noted that, in the British case, another advantage of part-time workers as far as employers are concerned is that they have been very cheap to employ. Employers do not have to pay National Insurance contributions for employees with weekly earnings below the lower earnings limit (£57 per week), and part-time employees have to take longer to accumulate employment protection rights than do full-time employees (note that recent EU legislation is likely to change this situation).

Part-time work, therefore, has a reputation of being insecure, low-paid, and with little by way of training or promotion prospects. Beechey and Perkins have argued that this is because part-time work is 'gendered', that is, it has been socially constructed as 'women's work' and paid accordingly:

Certain jobs . . . had been constructed as part-time jobs because they were seen to be women's jobs . . . (they) were invariably low graded, they were rarely defined as skilled even when they involved a range of competencies and responsibilities, women doing them lacked opportunities for promotion and training . . . and they were badly paid. The crucial fact to emerge from our research is that there is nothing *inherent* in the nature of particular jobs which makes them full-time or part-time. They have been constructed as such, and such constructions are closely related to gender. (Beechey and Perkins 1987: 145–6)

This argument suggests that it is *employers* who have systematically sought to create 'poor work' for women. Alternatively, it might be argued that this emphasis is not correct: rather, women have demanded part-time work to fit in with their domestic responsibilities, and employers have simply responded to this demand (Hakim 1996). We will return to this argument in a moment; but first we will briefly examine some recent evidence relating to the significance of part-time work in contributing to gender inequality (Rubery *et al.* 1994). This study found that part-time jobs *were* poorly paid in relation to full-time jobs, but when other differences (such as in skill levels) between part-time and full-time jobs were taken into account, female full-timers were not paid much more than female part-timers. In terms of pay, the major gap is between men and women, rather than between full-time and part-time employment.

Part-timers did not consider their jobs to be any more insecure than those of full-timers. However, only 29 per cent of part-timers thought their jobs offered promotion prospects, as compared to 52 per cent of women full-timers. In addition, the material differences between full-time and part-time work were much greater once work-related benefits—such as pension rights, insurance, sick pay, and other benefits such as meals and recreation facilities—had been taken into account. Rubery *et al.* also argue that the 'flexibility' offered by part-time work is arranged largely for the benefit of the employer. Part-time workers were less likely than full-time workers to have any choice over start and finish times, and over 50 per cent (a similar proportion to full-time workers) had no choice over the number of hours they worked. On the general question of flexibility, they suggest that:

The overall picture is ... one where full- and part-time jobs are associated with different types of flexibility. Full-time jobs, both male and female, are associated with working late and taking work home on the one hand, while part-time jobs involve weekend and evening work and variable days. (Rubery *et al.* 1994: 223)

They also suggest that there is a polarization between part-time jobs which require weekend work and those which do not. This is seen as a further refinement of the *employer's* strategy in respect of the 'flexible' labour force.

Rubery *et al.*'s findings suggest that it is largely in relation to employment-related benefits and opportunities for promotion, rather than pay or job security, that women's part-time work is inferior to full-time work. They also suggest that it is largely the employer's requirements which shape not only the demand for part-time work but also different kinds of part-time work. Their results, therefore, suggest that part-time work is not only of inferior quality, but has also been developed mainly to suit the needs of the employer.

Nevertheless, a major national survey (the Labour Force Survey) has consistently over the last ten years shown that the vast majority (over 80 per cent) of married women in part-time work gave as their major reason for being in such work the fact that they did not want a full-time job (Beatson 1995b: 16). Other surveys have found that part-time workers are also very likely to express themselves as 'satisfied' with their jobs. Indeed, this was also a feature of the part-time workers in Rubery *et al.*'s study (female part-timers had an average satisfaction score of 8.6, compared to 8.3 amongst female full-timers). If women have apparently chosen to work part-time, and express themselves as satisfied with their work, then indeed it might be argued that, rather than the employers 'designing' inferior part-time work for women, as Beechey and Perkins have asserted, they are simply responding to a demand from women for part-time work, as Hakim (1996) has argued.

In practice, both employer demand and women's preferences are important in explaining the growth of part-time work amongst women. We have to remember, however, that women's 'preferences' will be shaped by their available options, and it has often been pointed out that, as Britain has the lowest level of state (national or local) provision of childcare in Europe (Phillips and Moss 1988), then it is very likely that women with caring responsibilities will have a 'preference' for part-time work. Similarly, expressions of 'satisfaction' with a job do not identify exactly which aspects of the job are contributing to this satisfaction. If convenience of hours are most important to the worker, then the employee is likely to say they are 'satisfied' with part-time work. Rubery *et al.*'s study found that although the part-time women employees were more likely to say they were satisfied with their work, they were less likely to say that their current job was the job they 'had liked the best' out of all of their jobs than were full-timers. More than half of the part-timers also said that their qualifications might lead them to expect a better job than the one they had, as compared to only a third of the full-timers who thought this. These figures suggest that a substantial minority of part-time workers are under-employed, despite the apparently high level of satisfaction amongst this group. This kind of evidence should also make us conscious of the heterogeneity of the part-time female labour force.

Women who are employed part-time are likely to be giving a high priority to their domestic commitments, but they are nevertheless going '*out* to work'. This is in contrast to the other major type of 'feminized' employment which we will consider in this chapter—homeworking.

Homeworking

The 1991 Census counted 1.2 million people who worked 'mainly at home'—although, as we shall see, precise figures are very difficult to establish because definitions of 'homeworking' vary so much. Although homeworking makes up only a small proportion of people in employment, it has been of considerable interests to feminist sociologists because its persistence in Britain (and other countries) belied the common assumption that 'home' and work as employment have been separated as a consequence of the Industrial Revolution and the growth of factory production (Allen and Wolkowitz 1987).

Manufacturing homeworking (or 'outworking') had acquired a poor reputation as a component of the 'sweated trades', in which women and families took in sewing, assembled small items such as jewellery or parts of larger items, made matchboxes, or packed shirts, handkerchiefs and so on for an employer who supplied the work and collected the finished output. Such work was usually very badly paid, carried out in the cramped and unhealthy conditions of the working-class home, and offered little by way of social protections or security. These forms of employment were widely assumed to have gone into decline as a consequence of social reforms and rising living standards, and in 1978 a history of the sweated trades in the eighteenth and nineteenth centuries concluded: 'Outwork is rightly relegated to one of the darkest chapters of economic history; and now that it is virtually dead, none should regret its passing' (Bythell, quoted in Allen and Wolkowitz 1987).

However, it has been argued that, rather than disappearing, manufacturing homeworking has persisted throughout the twentieth century. Its apparent disappearance has in reality been but a reflection of its highly unofficial and subterranean nature, making it very unlikely to be picked up by official surveys. Women doing homeworking might be earning money 'off the cards' (that is, not declaring their income for tax or insurance purposes). They might be concerned about their liability for expensive overheads relating to official health and safety regulations, or consider that their activities are just too marginal to be worth recording. Thus the real extent of homeworking has been persistently under-reported. As we shall see, the difficulties of defining and researching homeworking are so complex that it is very difficult to be accurate as far as measurement is concerned, but there does seem to be good evidence of under-reporting amongst particular groups of homeworkers, including ethnic minorities.[1]

Homeworking, therefore, has not had a particularly good 'image'. In recent years, however, it has been argued that the nature of contemporary homeworking has been undergoing a radical transformation. It has been argued that traditional manufacturing homework has been 'supplemented and overtaken' by white-collar homework: 'professional, artistic and clerical work carried out as a personal or family business or undertaken for employers on variable contractual terms' (Hakim 1996: 36). This expansion has followed upon the technological revolution associated with the development of IT and computer technology, which has made possible both the development of the 'home office' and of 'teleworking'—that is, work carried out via a modem or computer link. Optimistic accounts of these developments point to the re-integration of work and home and its positive aspects—the possibility for both parents to be more involved in the care of their children, the energy savings on travel to work, and so on. The 'electronic cottage' is seen to be the workplace of the future.

The actual picture is highly diverse. As mentioned already, it is complicated by problems of both definition and measurement. For example, a self-employed plumber, a publican, or a General Practitioner might all work from home, but are they 'homeworkers'? Is a freelance journalist or author a 'homeworker', or would they be better considered as 'self-employed'? Do unpaid family workers count as homeworkers or not?

Hakim uses the term 'home-based workforce' to describe people working *at* home *and* people working *from* home. On this basis, the 'home-based workforce' in fact includes more men than women, and GPs, lawyers, and women packing disposable nappies would be in the same broad category. Thus those working *at* home and *from* home are usually distinguished from each other, but a further complication is introduced by the fact that the Census—which offers an estimate of 'people who work mainly *at* home'—includes in this category those who work in the same grounds and buildings as home. This would include the GP and the publican (Felstead and Jewson 1996). On this broad definition, the 1991 Census counted 1.2 million people who worked 'mainly at home'. This included people working in the same grounds and buildings as home, but not the self-employed plumber who did not actually work at home.

The most recent DfEE survey (Felstead and Jewson 1996) uses a narrow definition of homeworking: 'people who carry out paid work *in* their own home (not from home as a base) and are working in manufacturing or lower-level service sector jobs (such as inputting data)'. This narrow definition does not include people in professional or creative occupations such as journalists or lawyers, nor 'person-to-person trading'—for example, childminders. On this narrow definition, Felstead estimates that there are today 300,000 homeworkers, as compared to 100,000 in 1981. Rather than being 'virtually dead', it would appear that low-level homework is on the increase.

Official surveys tend to under-estimate homeworking for a number of reasons. Ethnic-minority homeworkers can often only be located by interviewers with specialist language skills. Women paid in cash are likely not to want to discuss their earnings if the household is in receipt of benefits. Workers themselves may be unsure of their status—are they employed or self-employed, for example? Because this is such a 'grey area' as far as official statistics are concerned, the only certain way of establishing the number of homeworkers in any particular area seems to be to go from house to house knocking on doors. Here again, researchers tend not to agree with each other as far as definitions are concerned. The only area of agreement amongst researchers would seem to be that such specialized surveys usually discover more homeworkers than had previously been thought to be present.

Studies of homeworking have revealed that lower-level homeworkers are almost invariably women. These studies also suggest that homeworking is not particularly well paid. The survey of homeworkers using the 'narrow' definition described above found that the mean hourly rate for homeworkers was £3.03, and the average number of hours worked was 32. However, these average figures cover a very wide range. Phizacklea and Wolkowitz's (1995) study found that the gender and ethnic inequalities in the wider society were mapped on to employment in homeworking. Thus clerical homeworkers got paid more than homeworkers in manual jobs, and white women tended to get paid more than women from ethnic minority groups. Their survey of homeworkers in Coventry found that non-manual homeworkers (coding, telecontact, and so on) were paid £3.14 an hour, not much less than the average for part-time non-manual workers (£3.20 in 1989), but there were no ethnic-minority women amongst the non-manual homeworkers. The survey also found that manual homework in Coventry was divided along ethnic lines. All of the Asian women did clothing assembly or other low-paid assembly work, and their earnings were concentrated in a narrow range, two-thirds earning between 75p and £1.50 an hour. In contrast, the jobs the white homeworkers did were more diverse (electrical assembling, craft knitting), and their earnings were more spread out across the range. Asian women were likely to work the equivalent of full-time hours, and their earnings, although meagre, were central to their household's economy.

A majority of homeworkers value the flexibility and autonomy that homework allows, and Felstead and Jewson's survey found that 64 per cent of the homeworkers they interviewed said that the chief advantage of homework was the opportunities it gave for looking after children. Not all homeworkers are living on the margin of existence, and a postal survey carried out by Phizacklea and Wolkowitz revealed a relatively high proportion of craft and clerical, as well as professional and managerial workers. Many of these women were very positive about the advantages of homework, particularly its flexibility in relation to childcare. As with part-time work, therefore, in the case of homework we seem to have another example of women being positively favourably disposed towards what might be thought of as 'objectively' poor conditions of employment. Hakim (1991; 1996) has argued that: 'The paradox of women's . . . apparently non-rational satisfaction with the worst jobs is highlighted in the extreme case of homework, which is found in all countries and is almost universally done by women only' (1991: 103). As we have seen in the first chapter, Hakim argued that this is because such women have chosen to put their families first and are therefore 'satisfied' with poor work (Hakim describes them as 'grateful slaves').

Whilst not denying that women do value the opportunity to earn money whilst looking after their children, nor that they appreciate the advantages of flexibility, we have to be careful about assuming that, as homeworking is a matter of 'choice', its consequences are all beneficial and the women in question have no complaints. Even women who say that they are happy or satisfied with their working arrangements are not necessarily happy with other aspects of the job. Even 'middle-class' homeworkers can be very critical of their level of pay (Phizacklea and Wolkowitz 1995), and other surveys of homeworkers have revealed similar discontents (Felstead and Jewson 1996).[2] It may also be noted that, as with part-time work, homeworkers lose (even more of) the benefits associated with full-time work, such as sick pay, pensions, holidays, and so on. In addition, they have to pay for their working costs, such as heating, electricity, and wear and tear on their furniture. It is not difficult to argue, therefore, that although women may value the convenience of homeworking, employers are obtaining labour at very low rates, for which they pay no overheads whatsoever (Allen and Wolkowitz 1987). More generally, the question should be raised as to why women should have to pay an employment penalty for the fact that they usually assume the main responsibility for the care of children— and usually other family members as well.

In the two cases of 'flexible' employment we have looked at, therefore (part-time employment and homeworking), this employment has been positively valued by the women concerned, but has nevertheless carried with it a number of disadvantages as compared to full-time, 'standard' work. These include lower rates of pay, few opportunities for promotion, and a loss of work-related benefits such as sick pay and pensions. Nevertheless, a range of factors are increasing the likelihood that 'flexible' employment will continue to increase. These are the political and economic pressures towards the creation of a 'flexible' labour force, technological developments facilitating the 'remote office', environmental concerns, and so on. As we have noted, the structure of men's flexible employment in Britain is rather different from that of women's. Men are more likely to be self-employed than to be part-timers, for example. There have been few studies which have actually compared men and women doing the same kind of 'flexible' work. Studies of newer forms of homeworking—'teleworking'—, however, suggests that men's attitudes and approach to homeworking are very different from those of women.

'Teleworking'—working at a computer or modem link—is a relatively superior form of 'homework'. The kind of work involved, however, varies considerably. It could be extremely routine data inputting on the one hand, or work incorporating a high level of professional and technical skills on the other—and it is likely that the distribution of different kinds of telework will itself be gendered. Phizacklea and Wolkowitz studied different kinds of teleworkers (all women), and it was very apparent that the employment terms of routine data-entry employees (low-level electronic homeworkers) were very different than those of the professionals (high-level electronic homeworkers). As they conclude, 'technology does not in itself guarantee a more agreeable, autonomous or better rewarded way of working at home unless the skills and experience that a particular worker combines with that technology are in short supply' (1995: 122).

Studies have revealed that men and women teleworkers have very different views on its advantages and disadvantages. A study of male computer professionals (Olsen, cited in Phizacklea and Wolkowitz 1995: ch. 5) showed that men's main reasons for teleworking were 'to increase my productivity' or 'to work in my own way'. In contrast, women overwhelmingly stress the *domestic* advantages—for example, a study of teleworking showed that 74 per cent of the women, but only 7 per cent of the men, rated the ability to look after children or dependents as a 'very important' advantage of homeworking. A small-scale study of men and women teleworkers cited by Phizacklea and Wolkowitz reflected the same gender contrast: the things men value about working at home is the personal autonomy it brings, the thing women value is its 'domestic' flexibility.

Manufacturing homeworking and the sweated trades have had, and still have a poor reputation, offering poor rates of pay for what are often very long hours of work (the Asian women in Phizacklea and Wolkowitz's Coventry sample averaged 48 hours a week). It is predominantly 'women's work', and although some researchers have argued that it is in decline, others consider it to be on the increase. Newer forms of homework associated with telework and the electronic cottage have a better reputation, and indeed what evidence there is suggests that it is likely to be better paid, and to include highly trained, professional people. It might also have been thought that the development of these newer forms of homeworking might be one area in which gender differences in employment might disappear. There is no intrinsic reason why the relationship of men and women to modems and computer screens might be any different. However, it would seem that gender differences are reflected in these newer forms of homeworking, both in the kinds of work men and women do, and the reasons they give for doing it.

The persistence of homeworking serves to remind us that women, particularly working-class women, have always done paid work, even when the home and paid work were supposedly divided from each other. Nevertheless, the numbers of women, particularly married women, taking up paid work outside the home have risen substantially during this century, and paid work has become much more important in the lives of most women. As we have seen, however, the structure of women's employment is different from men's. Another feature which some people would consider to be even more important is that women and men do not do the same jobs. In the next section of this chapter, therefore, we will consider this phenomenon—occupational segregation—in more depth.

Occupational Segregation

As discussed in Chapter 1, it has always been the case that some jobs are regarded as 'men's' jobs, and other jobs as 'women's' jobs. The is known as the 'sex-typing' of jobs and occupations. Ideas about 'suitable' jobs for men and women have reflected prevailing notions of manhood and womanhood, of masculinity and femininity. Thus, for example, with the coming of the Industrial Revolution 'woman's work' was seen as requiring high levels of dexterity and patience but little by way of skill and creativity, reflecting the assumption that women did not possess the drive or intellectual strengths of men, but nevertheless surpassed men in their docility, patience, and attention to detail (Bradley 1989). Ideas about 'suitable' (that is, gendered) jobs have varied over time and between countries—for example, in this country a hotel receptionist's job is thought of as female, whereas in the Far Eastern countries receptionists are all men. Once a job has become sex-typed, its identification is remarkably diffcult to change—a male secretary or personal assistant, for example, would be seen as rather out-of-place even today.

The sex-typing of jobs is a major factor contributing to occupational segregation. Hakim (1979) has described occupational segregation as follows:

> occupational segregation by gender exists when men and women do different kinds of work, so that one can speak of two separate labour forces, one male and one female, which are not in competition with each other for the same jobs. (1979: 1)

In practice, complete segregation—that is, two separate male and female labour forces—is not known at the societal level. However, it is not difficult to find particular examples of separate labour forces from traditional industries. For example, in the British shoe industry, 'clicking' (cutting the leather) was a man's job, whereas 'closing' (machining shoe uppers) was a woman's job.

Occupational segregation has received a lot of attention from academics and policy-making bodies because it has been seen as a major factor explaining the persisting material inequality between men and women. In Britain in the 1970s, laws were passed which made it illegal to pay women less than men for doing the same job. However, despite this move towards equal pay, the wage gap between men and women persisted, and today whilst the mean hourly earnings of full-time manual men is 670p, women earn 481p (the mean hourly rate for full-time non-manual men is 1183p, and for women, 816p. *Source*: New Earnings Survey, 1996). Occupational segregation—the fact that men and women do different jobs—is considered to explain much of the gender wage gap.[3] This is because jobs where there are many (or only) women tend to be poorly paid, often because they are considered to be 'women's jobs', and women's skills are undervalued. Thus reducing the level of occupational segregation has been considered to be an important objective in achieving equality for women, in that it would mean that women had gained access to these 'better' jobs.

There are a number of different measures of occupational segregation, which give a useful summary indication of the job/gender structure. The differences between the different measures can get very technical, but ratios are very commonly used as an index. These indexes are based on comparing the sex-ratio (that is, the proportion of men to women) within each occupation with the sex-ratio of the labour force as a whole (Hakim 1979). Thus, if women were found in an occupation in exactly the same proportion as their representation in the labour force (that is, for example, if women were 40 per cent of the labour force and also 40 per cent of an occupation), the index would be 1, no segregation. A measure of more than 1 would mean that women were over-represented in that occupation, a measure of less than 1 would mean that women were under-represented. Extreme care, however, must be taken in using measures of occupational segregation in arguments and evidence. For example, it has been well-established that the more detailed the level of the occupational classification, the more likely men are to work mainly with men and women to work mainly with women. Thus the more comprehensive and detailed the classification, the more likely are high levels of segregation to be identified and measured. For example, if we return to the example of the footwear industry cited above, if the proportion of women in the closing 'room' was 40 per cent of the footwear workforce and the proportion of women in the labour force as a whole was also 40 per cent, then the general category of 'footwear worker' would have an index of 1—no segregation—even though the men and women in the industry would be doing completely different jobs.

In any case, because men and women are, after all, 'different', it would be very unlikely for them to be distributed in the labour force in exactly the same jobs. The crux of the matter, however, lies in the fact that the jobs in which women are concentrated tend to be those which are poorly paid. That is, 'difference' seems to be, almost inevitably, associated with hierarchy, in the field of employment as much as anywhere else. As we have seen in Chapter 1, this has been a recurring problem for those who have sought equality for women with men.

Hakim (1979) has distinguished two aspects of segregation: *horizontal segregation*, when men and women are concentrated in different types of work, and *vertical segregation*, where men are concentrated in higher and women in lower grades, both within and between occupations and industries. Horizontal segregation means that men and women do different jobs, vertical segregation means that they are at higher and lower levels within the same job or occupational structure. This apparently simple distinction can in fact be problematic, as the job or occupational structure is simultaneously functionally *and* hierarchically differentiated, and it is not always a straightforward matter to sort out the two. For example, 'clerks' and 'managers' are classified as different occupations, but 'clerks' are also subordinate to 'managers'.[4] Does the fact that women are a majority of those in clerical occupations reflect horizontal or vertical segregation? In practice, an answer to this question would have to take into account whether or not clerical jobs were linked to managerial jobs in a promotion hierarchy.

The fact that there are a number of processes contributing to the job/gender distribution outcome is another reason why summary measures of segregation should be used with care. For example, in the Scandinavian countries, women are concentrated in the caring professions associated with welfare-state provision, but these jobs are well-paid. This means that indices show a high level of occupational segregation by sex, but because 'women's' jobs are well paid, the gender wage gap is a relatively narrow one in these countries (as we shall see in Chapter 3). In short, as far as women's equality is concerned, for practical purposes the problem is not so much occupational segregation as such, but the fact that women are poorly paid for what they do. As pay is usually associated with hierarchy, then, as Hakim (1992) has argued, it is vertical segregation which is the key issue in relation to women's equality.

Another strategy relates to the notion of *equal value*. This approach directly challenges the cultural 'downgrading' of women's jobs, and seeks to extend the principle of 'equal pay for equal work' to 'equal pay for work of *equal value*'. The Equal Opportunities Commission (EOC) has pursued a number of such cases, and sometimes their outcomes can be quite dramatic, such as the recent decision by Marks and Spencer and Sainsbury's to increase the level of pay for their checkout operators after another case had found that such work was of equal value to that of warehouse employees.

The broad picture of occupational segregation by sex will be familiar to everyone. Four occupational categories (clerical occupations, secretarial occupations, personal services occupations, and 'other elementary' occupations) accounted for over half of all employment for women in 1991. In contrast, the same four categories accounted for just 17 per cent of male employment (Wilson 1994). Women tend to predominate in 'caring' occupations such as looking after old people and children, in 'domestic' jobs such as cleaning, in unskilled manual and lower-level clerical work, in the 'lower' professions (such as teaching and nursing) rather then the higher (such as professors and architects), and in occupations supporting management rather than higher-level or corporate management.

There have, of course, been many changes in recent years—for example, separate entrances and staircases for female clerks, to spare them the attentions of male clerks (Crompton 1988), are no longer considered necessary! Nevertheless, in a recent survey, 66 per cent of men said they worked exclusively or mainly with men, and 54 per cent of women said they worked exclusively or mainly with women (Scott ed. 1994). The survey found that gender segregation was related to both occupational class and industry. Segregation was higher in manual than in non-manual work, and higher in manufacturing industry than in services. Pay data showed that men earned more than women in each occupational class, but that men's earnings were even higher when they worked in 'men's' jobs, illustrating the effect that segregation has on pay levels.

Table 2.1 Women's representation in major occupational groups, 1979, 1990

	1979	1990
Professional and related supporting management and administration	0.52	0.66
Professional and related in education, welfare and health	1.62	1.56
Literary, artistic, and sport	0.84	0.94
Professional and related in science, engineering and technology	0.23	0.29
Managerial: large and small establishments	0.53	0.65
Clerical and related	1.85	1.79
Selling	1.53	1.38
Security and protective service	0.25	0.27
Catering, cleaning, hairdressing and other personal service	2.07	1.84
Farming, fishing and related	0.34	0.51
Processing, making, repairing, and related (not metal and electrical)	0.87	0.68
Processing, making, repairing, and related (metal and electrical)	0.13	0.12
Painting, repetitive assembly, product inspection, packaging, etc.	1.17	0.93
Construction, mining, and related	0.01	0.02
Transport operating, materials moving, storing, and related	0.14	0.15
Miscellaneous	0.19	0.18
Not stated or occupation unclear	1.42	0.28

Source: derived from Hakim (1992: Table 3)

In 1979, Hakim's review of occupational segregation concluded that:

occupational segregation (has) remained relatively unchanged in Britain over seven decades. The types of occupation in which women or men are over- or under-represented have changed somewhat, with women increasingly forming the majority of the labour force in the lowest grade of white-collar and blue-collar work, very often in occupations which closely mirror functions carried out on an unpaid basis in the home. (p. 34)

This broad picture still characterizes the occupational structure in the 1990s, but as Table 2.1 demonstrates, recent trends show important changes. This table gives details of the coefficients of female re-presentation in major occupational groups, a measure similar to the sex ratio. It is obtained by dividing the female share of employment in the occupations in question by the female share of total employment. Thus a figure greater than 1 indicates women's over-representation in an occupation, while a figure below 1 indicates their under-representation.

It can be seen that, during the 1980s, women's over-representation in lower-grade and less well-paid occupations has been reduced, and their representation in professional and managerial occupations has increased. More men are now in service occupations—catering, cleaning, hairdressing, and so on—in sales, and in lower-level clerical work. Men still remain very dominant in areas such as mining and metal and electric manufacture (where there have also been massive job losses during the period in question), as well as in construction and transport. However, women have increased their representation in professional jobs, particularly management. Even in the 1970s, women were well- (indeed, over-) represented in the health and welfare professions, but during the 1980s they have moved increasingly into management and management-related professions and occupations.

The increased entry of women into management and the professions has run in parallel with both changes in legislation (for example, Equal Opportunities legislation, which made practices such as low female quotas for entry into medical school illegal) and the increasing levels of academic and vocational qualifications obtained by young women (Crompton 1992; Crompton and Sanderson 1986). Women are now a slight majority of those gaining entry into medical school, and have also moved rapidly into other professions, such as law and accountancy. In some occupations the change in gender composition over the last twenty-five years has been quite dramatic—for example, from 4 per cent to 27 per cent of 'judges, advocates, barristers, and solicitors', and from 20 per cent to 51 per cent of administrative and executive local government officers between 1971 and 1990 (Hakim 1992). These kinds of changes reflect the fact that many women have sought to add to their 'human capital'—that is, as *individuals*, they have become better-qualified and therefore capable of moving into higher-level and professional jobs. In cases where women have decided to undertake difficult and long-term training for entry into the professions and similar occupations, it is appropriate to place a considerable emphasis upon their determination and motivation in explaining their behaviour, although this does not mean they will encounter no gendered barriers in employment, as we shall see in Chapter 5.

Although women might apparently be somewhat improving their occupational position in relation to men, overall the structure of women's employment is tending to polarize. Women are increasing their share of employment in managerial and professional jobs, but opportunities for the unskilled and/or unqualified are declining (as they are, indeed, for men). Recent projections suggest the possibility of a decline in the number of clerical jobs (Wilson 1994). This would be a serious matter, as clerical jobs are a very important middle-rank job for women. Another feature which should temper more optimistic predictions is that many of the managerial jobs in which women are located are in sales and the 'hospitality industry' (hotels and catering). Managerial jobs in these industries are often very low-paid (Rubery and Fagan 1994; Crompton and Sanderson 1990).

In Britain, therefore, men's work and women's work is still characterized by a considerable level of gender concentration, particularly as far as working-class men are concerned. The level of occupational segregation is becoming less pronounced, although men still predominate in higher-level, and women in lower-level, occupations. Vertical segregation—keeping women out of higher-level positions—is in the process of unravelling in some occupations. There have clearly been important changes over the last twenty years.

Summary and Conclusions

In this chapter, we have looked at the structure of women's employment in contemporary Britain. The major features that we would emphasise are:

- That the growth of women's paid employment, particularly since the Second World War, has been largely a growth of married women's employment.

- Much of this employment growth has been concentrated in 'non-standard' forms of employment—particularly part-time work.
- Women's domestic responsibilities are still very important in shaping the kind of work they do—particularly in the case of part-time work and other forms of non-standard employment such as homeworking (there is not much empirical evidence available, but men who work at home tend to do so for different reasons from women, stressing their personal autonomy needs rather than their domestic responsibilities).
- The broad contours of occupational segregation remain much as they always have been, but occupational segregation is becoming less pronounced and women are moving into some higher-level occupations.

We have also seen that despite the fact that non-standard employment, such as part-time work and homeworking, is often poorly paid, and has little or nothing by way of promotion prospects, or pension or other benefits, the majority of women doing this kind of work do not want to work full-time, and/or are highly appreciative of the domestic flexibility such employment gives them. It might be argued, therefore, that such women have chosen to take up this kind of employment, much as other women—particularly those moving into higher-level professions and occupations—have chosen to invest in the lengthy and expensive business of gaining qualifications and experience. In Hakim's terms, women homeworkers, and those in part-time jobs, are 'uncommitted' employees who put their domestic responsibilities first, whereas the women going into higher-level occupations are 'committed' to an employment, rather than a domestic, career.

Whilst these individualist explanations do have some validity, we have also indicated that they are not the whole story. Although part-time workers might be satisfied with their hours of work, there is also evidence which suggests that many are aware that the job itself does not match their actual capabilities—as, indeed, is often the case. Similarly, homeworkers express resentment at their low wages and at what is often the general inconvenience of homework—although they appreciate the advantages of being at home as far as matters such as childcare are concerned. Domestic considerations *may* be paramount as far as many women are concerned, but this does not mean that these women are satisfied with the negative aspects of their employment. Employers gain considerable advantages from the cheap and flexible labour provided by women, and we might raise the broader question as to why women should pay an employment quality 'penalty' for the fact that they have taken responsibility for caring and domestic work in the household.

There is a further factor to consider, also related to the particular circumstances faced by women in Britain. Britain has the lowest level of state-provided childcare in Europe. Women with children who wish to work full-time have had to make their own childcare arrangements, which in many cases are likely to be just too expensive in relation to the woman's likely income. This is likely to be an important constraint affecting British women's employment patterns.

In Chapter 3, therefore, we will examine comparatively the national institutional contexts within which women's employment patterns have been shaped. We shall see that, although there are important cross-national continuities in the structuring of women's employment, there are also significant variations, suggesting the continuing importance of structural factors.

Chapter Three

Cross-National Comparisons

Introduction: Women and State Policies

In Chapter 3 we examined in some detail the structure of paid work amongst women in Britain—the hours women work, the kinds of work they do—together with evidence relating to some important changes over the last few decades. In this chapter, we will turn our attention to the role of the state in these matters, which will also involve taking a look at the situation in other countries. We will also take this opportunity to begin to examine comparatively the other important aspect of 'women's work' which has so far not had a central place in our analyses: unpaid work or the work of caring. As we argued in Chapter 1, the gender division of labour—that is, 'men's' and 'women's' work— has always incorporated the differential allocation of domestic work, as well as market work, between the sexes.

State policies have obviously had an important impact on women's labour-market position and behaviour. For example, Equal Pay and Opportunities legislation had an immediate impact on women's pay levels in Britain. In the past, governments have intervened directly to prevent women taking up specific jobs—such as underground work in the mines—and have also restricted the times and hours of women's employment. As we saw in Chapter 1, Walby (1986) has argued that the direct intervention of the state in women's employment reflects the assumption of patriarchal control by the capitalist state. Walby (1990) makes these points as part of her larger argument that the nineteenth and twentieth centuries have seen a shift from 'private' to 'public' patriarchy, and that state control over women's conditions of employment has played a major part in this. Women, she argues, are today no longer confined to the domestic or 'private' sphere and controlled within it, but are segregated within the 'public' sphere of paid employment (through, for example, occupational segregation or inferior part-time work), and thus kept subordinate.

However, historically states have more usually focused on women's actual or potential roles as wives and mothers, rather than their rights as individuals and/or roles as workers. Nation states have always been concerned with the maintenance of their populations. Thus the question of fertility—that is, whether or not women have children—is crucial. If women do not bear children, then the state has no citizens and the employers no labour force. If there are too many people, then there is an increased likelihood of economic hardship or even starvation. Thus all contemporary nation states have, to varying degrees, enacted legislation in relation to motherhood and reproduction. Some states have sought to control the level of their populations—as, for example, in the 'one-child' policy in contemporary China. Other states, in contrast, have at various times encouraged women to have children, and have therefore developed 'pro-natalist' policies. As we shall see in our discussions of France and the Czech Republic, such policies have been very significant for women in these countries. The regulation of motherhood and reproduction—which make up a large part of women's unpaid work—will therefore have an important impact on the pattern of women's paid work.

Another closely related topic is public health, which became a major issue in nineteenth- and twentieth-century Britain. Obviously, the health of children was considered to be extremely important, and women as mothers were assumed to take the major responsibility for this. As we saw in Chapter 1, in Britain women's childcare responsibilities have until very recently been seen as taking precedence over their entitlement to paid employment. In Britain, 'good mothers' have been mothers who stayed at home with their children (Lewis 1980). Except in cases such as homeworking (discussed in Chapter 2), such mothers cannot also be engaged in paid work.

State policies in respect of mothers and children have not necessarily been *intentionally* structured so as to have a direct impact upon women's employment patterns. Rather, their impact is often indirect. However, as has been stressed in this book, the distribution of unpaid caring work between the sexes will crucially affect the capacities of both men and women to take up paid market work. Thus if the state (and other institutions) assign unpaid caring work largely to women, this will obviously affect their possibilities of employment. In all nation states, the identification of women with the caring role has resulted in many continuities between countries in the patterning of women's employment—particularly in relation to the kinds of jobs that women do (that is, occupational segregation). The tendency for women to be engaged more often than men in occupations linked to education, health, welfare, and caring for others would seem to be universal. The over-representation of women in lower-level occupations is also found to be the case across a wide range of countries.

However, different nation states have had different policies on the 'woman (and children) question', and as we shall see in this chapter, this is reflected in considerable variations in patterns of employment amongst women in different countries. In particular: (1) different welfare state 'regimes' have structured the broad pattern of women's employment in different ways; (2) there have also been national variations in the kinds of policies developed in pursuit of equality for women; and (3) states have also varied considerably in the extent and kinds of encouragement and support they have given to women as mothers, and this has also affected the structure of women's employment.

Cross-national comparisons are important for a number of reasons. They provide an empirical test of theories and explanations which have been developed with reference to experiences in a single country. They help us to understand and appreciate a major theme that we are developing in this book—that is, the significance of particular economic and social contexts in shaping women's employment patterns. A process of comparison also helps us to identify 'best practices' as far as policy developments—such as the pursuit of equal treatment for women—are concerned. We will begin our comparative exercise by examining in brief one major respect in which the structure of women's employment in Britain differs from that in many other countries—the extent of part-time work.

Cross-National Comparisons: Explaining the Difference

As we saw in Chapter 2, Britain has a high level of part-time working amongst women. Feminist authors such as Walby have argued that part-time work was a significant element in the twentieth-century compromise between patriarchs and capitalists which ensured that both groups had access to the labour of women. In the British case, the historical record does suggest that, particularly during the period of labour shortage in the decades following the Second World War, part-time work for women was indeed consciously developed so that women could fulfill their 'two roles' at home and work. However, the actual extent of part-time employment amongst women varies considerably between different countries. This suggests that even if Walby's explana-

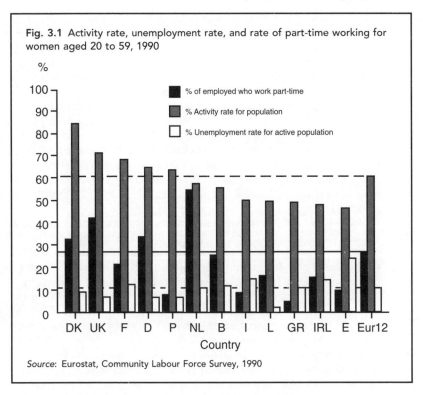

Fig. 3.1 Activity rate, unemployment rate, and rate of part-time working for women aged 20 to 59, 1990

% of employed who work part-time

% Activity rate for population

% Unemployment rate for active population

Country

Source: Eurostat, Community Labour Force Survey, 1990

tion does apply (in part) to the British situation, the same does not necessarily hold true for other countries.

Figure 3.1 describes the level of part-time work amongst women for a range of different countries.

It can be seen that the UK has one of the highest levels of part-time work in Europe, only the Netherlands having a greater proportion of part-time workers. Some countries—Greece, Portugal, Italy, Spain—have levels of part-time working well below the European average, and France, which might be thought of as a country very similar to Britain in many respects, has only half the level of part-time working amongst women as the UK.

How do we account for these variations in the level of part-time working amongst women in different countries? As with all such general questions, there will be no single answer, as different factors will have had an impact on different countries at different moments in time. In

Chapter 2, we have already seen how, in Britain, governments have effectively encouraged part-time employment by making such workers very cheap to employ, as the employer has not had to pay National Insurance contributions on low levels of part-time earnings. However, in other countries, such as France, part-time workers have been entitled to the same protections and benefits as full-time workers, making them relatively expensive to employ. In Spain, employment protections have been so highly developed that part-time work has not actually been officially allowed until relatively recently, and thus its recorded level—in official statistics at any rate—has been very low. Recorded levels of part-time work, therefore, will vary considerably depending upon how employment is regulated (that is, the rules and regulations concerning things like insurance, employment protection, and so on) in different countries.

It would not be correct, therefore, to regard the extent of part-time work amongst women only as reflecting the accommodation between capitalism and patriarchy, as has been suggested by authors such as Walby (1986) and Barrett and Mackintosh (1980). We saw in Chapter 1 that Hakim (1996) has used part-time working as a way of identifying 'uncommitted' women employees in Britain; but it would be difficult to argue, on this evidence, that levels of 'work commitment' amongst women in Europe vary to the extent that would seem to be suggested by Figure 3.1. Rather, as noted above, this empirical evidence of variation in levels of part-time work in different nation states may be used to emphasize the significance of particular social and economic contexts in the structuring of women's employment patterns. As Esping-Andersen has argued (1993: 8), important 'institutional filters' or regulatory mechanisms—welfare states, collective bargaining systems, educational systems, family policies, and so on—which vary considerably between different countries, have shaped national patterns of employment. This is no more true than in the case of women. Cross-national variations in women's employment patterns, therefore, reinforce our arguments concerning the significance of structural constraints, as well as individual choice, in shaping women's work. In the next section we will examine comparatively an institution which has been absolutely crucial as far as 'women's work' (in all senses) is concerned—the Welfare State.

Women's Employment and Welfare States

In this book we have stressed that, in contemporary societies, the structure of paid work in the market rests upon a parallel structure of unpaid work, largely but not entirely carried out by women, in the home or domestic sphere. Historically, the domestic sphere was once fully responsible for the caring for and social support of individuals. To a considerable extent, this is still the case today, but in modern societies these supports have to varying degrees been supplemented and enhanced by the state.

Some sort of non-family social provision, by church, parish, or charity, has been provided for the destitute since the beginning of modern times. In many circumstances, such as, for example, the system of Workhouses in Britain which followed from the 1834 Poor Law, relief was provided as an extremely unpleasant last resort, and was actively feared by the poor (see, for example, Humphries' account of the significance of the working-class family, discussed in Chapter 1). The organization of social provisions by States expanded during the first half of the twentieth century. For example, in Britain, old-age pensions were first introduced in 1908. After the Second World War, however, there took place in industrialized countries the widespread development of government policies which sought not just to relieve destitution, but also to intervene in the market—through, for example, systems of compulsory social insurance giving access to health care and pensions in old age, unemployment and invalidity benefits, and so on—in order to prevent extremes of poverty and destitution arising in the first place. These developments have been described as the coming of the 'welfare state'.

Gender differences were built into the structuring of the welfare state from the very beginning. Pateman (1989) has argued that whereas men were incorporated into the welfare state as individual citizens—that is, as workers who could contribute to social insurance—women were incorporated as members of families, that is, as wives and mothers. Men were employees or potential employees, heads of households or potential heads of households; women were dependents who made claims on the welfare state through their relationship as a member of an employee's household. Women were not, therefore, full 'citizens', as they did not have direct access to the provisions of social citizenship. As feminists have argued, the welfare state was constructed on the 'male-breadwinner' model of the family (Land 1994). For example, the author of the major report which shaped the British Welfare State (Beveridge 1942) wrote that 'the great majority of married women must be regarded as occupied on work which is vital though unpaid, without which their husbands could not do their paid work and without which the nation could not continue'. In the National Insurance Act of 1946 wives were treated differently from their husbands for insurance purposes. Married women, if they were working, paid lesser contributions for reduced benefits, and could even opt out of benefit payments on the assumption that they would be supported by their husbands (Pateman 1989: 194). Women's unpaid domestic work was, therefore, not regarded as making an independent (or 'productive') contribution worthy of social insurance.

Clearly, much has changed since welfare states were set up, and married women in Britain ceased to be able to opt out of benefits in 1975. The point that is being argued here is that welfare states were and are major institutions which have been consciously and unconsciously moulded so as to reflect prevailing assumptions concerning the division of labour between the sexes. At their inception, the 'male-breadwinner' model of the gender division of labour was dominant in most countries, and this was reflected in national welfare institutions. Welfare states have certainly been modified, but nevertheless, unpaid caring work, with some exceptions (particularly in Scandinavian countries, which we will be discussing in a later section of this chapter), does not carry with it insurance or benefit rights.

Systems of state welfare have developed in parallel with the expansion of married women's paid employment, which was described in Chapter 2. The post-war growth of welfare states has had an important and obvious impact. The expansion of education and health care, social insurance which cares for the old and sick, and so on simultaneously relieves women of some of their domestic duties and creates new paid jobs for women through the provision of these services in the wage economy. Welfare states vary considerably in the extent of the support they offer to their citizens, and this corresponds to different models of service provision.

The links between the development of different kinds of welfare states and related national patterns of women's employment are described in Esping-Andersen's (1990) characterization of different welfare-state 'regimes'. He has also linked his analysis of different welfare-state developments to a broader account of the emergence of 'post-industrial' society, which he sees as leading to important changes in the division of labour between men and women (ed. Esping-Andersen 1993). Esping-Andersen (1990) has identified three different clusters of welfare state regimes.

The *social democratic* regime cluster represents the Scandinavian welfare states. Such welfare states are universalistic, and all citizens are entitled to a high level of state-provided social supports. This corresponds to the 'rights-based' model, and as everybody is entitled to the same benefits, such states have an egalitarian (equalising) impact. The *corporatist* regime cluster is based upon insurance rights (corresponding to the 'insurance-based' model). Unlike universal or social democratic welfare states, in corporatist welfare states not everybody gets the same level of welfare benefits, as the levels of social insurance (and benefits) reflect wage and salary inequalities. In these circumstances, the welfare state does not have a redistributive or equalizing impact, but welfare levels are good and there is little incentive to move outside the state system (Austria, France, Germany, and Italy are examples of corporatist welfare states). In contrast, in *liberal* (or residual) welfare states, welfare benefits are means-tested and only provided for those in greatest need. Because the state only provides a minimum, a market develops—and may even be encouraged—for the private provision of welfare needs (private health care, pension plans, and so on). The United States is a major example of such a welfare state, although since 1979 Britain has moved much closer to this model, and may now be considered to be a 'liberal' welfare state.

A central concept in Esping-Andersen's analysis of welfare states is that of '*de-commodification*'. In most modern societies most people are directly or indirectly dependent upon the sale of labour—that is, working for a wage. 'De-commodification' occurs when a person can maintain a livelihood without reliance on the market; that is, without necessarily having to have a paid job. Welfare states vary in the extent to which 'de-commodification' has been achieved. In liberal welfare states, the relatively low and means-tested nature of the benefits means that not much is achieved by way of de-commodification. This situation is reflected in the greater reliance on 'market forces' in these states. As we saw in Chapter 2, 'market forces' also generate more relatively low-level, non-standard, part-time employment as well. Social democratic or Scandinavian welfare states are the most de-commodifying, in that a reasonable level of benefit is made available to all citizens. Corporatist social insurance schemes give good benefits, but the individual remains tied to employment. Thus on the de-commodification scale, corporatist welfare states lie in-between social democratic and liberal welfare states.

Esping-Andersen links his welfare-state typology to the emergence and development of 'post-industrial' societies. In using the concept of 'post-industrial' societies, he is describing the widespread move from economies dominated by employment in large-scale organizations and manufacturing industry, which he calls 'fordist' economies,[1] to those dominated by service employment. In most countries (particularly Scandinavia), welfare states have played a major role in the creation of service employment. Esping-Andersen argues that 'post-industrial' economies are replacing the 'fordist' model of manufacturing industry (in Chapter 2, we noted the increasing domination of services in the British occupational structure, from 36 per cent manufacturing and 53 per cent service employment in 1971 to 20 per cent in manufacturing and 73 per cent in services in 1993). The 'fordist' model was grounded in the 'male-breadwinner' model of the gender division of labour (which we have discussed extensively in previous chapters), in which a 'standard wage' male employee is supposed to support a non-employed wife and family. As we have seen in our discussion of the British welfare state, these were certainly the assumptions which prevailed in Britain in the 1940s and 1950s. Esping-Andersen's argument, therefore, is of interest here because he is a major theorist who has attempted to suggest what kinds of restructured 'male-breadwinner' employment models might be emerging.

Esping-Andersen argues that no single post-industrial model is emerging, in that different welfare states are associated with different post-industrial economies. In making his argument Esping-Andersen compares three societies with different systems of state welfare: Sweden (social democratic), Germany (corporatist), and the United States (liberal). In Sweden, post-industrialism has been associated with the expansion of highly professionalized welfare-state employment. In Germany, service employment has not expanded to the same extent, and in the United States, there has been an expansion not only of business-related professional services, but also an explosion of unqualified service jobs. How does women's employment relate to these three models? Sweden is extreme in that the welfare state is committed to social services, and the expansion of social-welfare services in the public sector has dominated women's employment.[2] Jobs are of relatively high quality, and women account for 87 per cent of total health–education–welfare employment growth in Sweden (Esping-Andersen 1990: 202). Women's continuing attachment to employment is supported through generous maternity leaves, and most women pursue uninterrupted employment careers. Thus women dominate in the post-industrial (service) hierarchy, and men in the fordist (industrial) hierarchy: the job hierarchy is segregated, but women are in relatively superior state service jobs.

Insurance-based corporatist welfare states such as Germany exclude non-working wives, and the way in which benefits are paid assumes they will actually be physically provided within the family: 'In the German nexus the social-welfare component of post-industrialism hardly grew, allowing only a modest level of welfare-state absorption of women workers . . . the German state remains a male domain, and women stay at home' (Esping-Andersen 1990: 202). Esping-Anderson sees Germany as a relatively retarded post-industrial society, still dominated by manufacturing. In the American case, government is more of a passive force, and the market has been relied upon to create jobs. Low wages have been the major source of service job growth. Women have moved into both the 'good' as well as the 'bad' jobs which have been created. Despite these cross-national variations, however, Esping-Andersen argues that there are a number of cross-national similarities:

the service economy is everywhere associated with the evolution of two gendered labour markets. Except for routine administrative and sales jobs, the traditional fordist economy remains predominantly male. The evolving services are becoming a women's labour market. It is hardly an exaggeration to say that the post-industrial economy, as we have defined it, is a female economy; in the United States, the female bias is modest (and in decline), but in Scandinavia it is extreme. (1993: 236)

The sweep of Esping-Andersen's argument is extremely broad, and, as we shall see, it is not at all difficult to locate individual examples of deviations from the patterns he describes. Some of his major concepts are also rather contentious—for example, it is not clear that all industrial societies can be described as 'fordist'. However, his argument is a useful organizing framework within which to begin to describe changing patterns of contemporary employment, especially as they relate to gender.[3] As we have seen, Esping-Andersen's argument does take on board some major feminist arguments—notably his identification of the importance of the 'male-breadwinner' model in the shaping of important contemporary institutions, and the significance of its decline.

However, feminists have argued that his analysis may be criticized because it has only focused upon paid work, and takes no systematic account of non-market or caring work. Jane Lewis has argued that 'women can only enter Esping-Andersen's analysis when they enter the paid labour market' (1993: 14). This point also relates to another of Esping-Andersen's central concepts: that of 'de-commodification'. As we have seen, this identifies the extent to which workers may be said to be independent of the market, and de-commodification is described by Esping-Anderson in a very positive light. Indeed, one criterion by which the 'success' of welfare states is evaluated is the extent to which 'de-commodification' has been achieved. However, much of women's labour (particularly caring work) is not strictly commodified in that it is not directly marketed, but carried out within the domestic sphere.

Women's work, therefore, may not be 'commodified', but this 'de-commodification' is usually associated with *dependence* (on a partner, or state benefits), rather than independence (Lister 1992). Except in universalist welfare states, people who have not contributed to social insurance through employment usually have to rely on second-class social assistance benefits requiring no contribution record: this would include divorced and deserted women, as well as unmarried mothers.

O'Connor (1993), therefore, has suggested that the concept of 'decommodification' should be supplemented by that of personal *autonomy*, that is, the extent to which the individual is insulated from personal and/or public dependence, and that the effectiveness of welfare states should be judged by the extent to which this autonomy has been achieved, as well as the de-commodification principle. As we have seen, personal autonomy for the majority of adults in contemporary industrial societies is closely linked to whether or not the individual gains an (independent) income from the work that they do, as well as the extent of this income. We have argued that 'work' may be carried out in the public sphere as paid employment, or in the private sphere—that is, caring and domestic work. It may be suggested that the personal autonomy of women will be greater both in the extent to which their wages in the public sphere are equivalent to those of men, and in the extent to which there is some kind of official recognition of the value of caring work in the private sphere. This second dimension, of course, reflects the feminist critique of 'orthodox' accounts of work and the labour-market theories which we have been developing in this book.

Initially, welfare states as such did not include women's unpaid work for insurance purposes—although, as we shall see, this is changing in some countries. One way in which states have given a material value to some of this work, however, is by offering women inducements to have children: that is, through the development of pro-natalist policies. Such inducements, however, have emphasized women's 'traditional' roles as mothers, rather than their roles as workers. Although the mother's role is a vital one to society, historically it has not been seen as one meriting full social citizenship, as the way in which social insurance and welfare states were developed suggests. Nevertheless, the availability of facilities for mothers—such as childcare, for example—will affect their capacities to be workers and thus become full 'citizens'. In any case, if the arguments relating to the increasing significance of paid employment for women in post-industrial economies are valid, women are becoming increasingly defined as 'workers', as well as mothers.

We will illustrate these arguments by drawing upon comparative evidence from four countries: the UK, France, Norway, and the Czech Republic. Extending our analysis to an ex-state-socialist country (the Czech Republic) adds to our arguments relating to the importance of focusing upon both unpaid work *and* paid employment when discussing 'women's work', and of recognizing their interdependence. After the Soviet (that is, Russian)-dominated 'revolutions' in Eastern Europe, there developed in the Soviet-bloc countries national worker- and productivist-dominated ideologies in which priority was given to material production. Within this framework, women were seen to have been 'liberated' if they took part in production outside the home—that is, if they became workers. State socialist ideology, therefore, proclaimed a formal equality for women in the world of employment, but did not systematically seek to transform the domestic division of labour in the home. This has had a very negative impact on the stated objective of the Soviet state—that of achieving equality for women—as gender relations have remained very conventional as a consequence (see Lapidus, discussed in Bradley 1989).

Cross-National Comparisons: Britain, France, Norway, and the Czech Republic

In our discussions so far, we have identified two major dimensions of state policy which might be expected to have a significant impact on the structuring of women's employment patterns. These are:

- The history and nature of the system of state-organised welfare (the 'welfare state').
- The nature (or absence) of the state's role in supporting women's unpaid work, in particular that of mothers.

If such supports do exist, it is significant whether they have come about as aspects of pronatalist policies, which have emphasized women's roles as mothers, or as aspects of an 'equality agenda', which are more likely to emphasize their roles as workers. Thus we would add that a third important aspect of state policy is the nature of the state's role in promoting equality for women (the 'equality agenda').

Our discussion of women's employment in the four countries will focus upon each of these aspects. In this short chapter, our discussion cannot be comprehensive. Nevertheless, it will give valuable insights into the complex structuring of women's employment in different nation states.

State-Organized Welfare

Britain

The modern British welfare state was set up in 1946, on a combination of universal and social insurance principles. As we have seen, it was in the beginning an explicitly 'male-breadwinner' welfare state. However, since the 1970s the British welfare state has been 'rolled back' and benefits have been reduced and increasingly means-tested. It would now be considered as a 'liberal' welfare state. As in the Esping-Andersen model, these developments have resulted in an expansion of relatively low level service work for women. The privatization of state services (such as hospital cleaning or the school meals service) has in fact resulted in an explosion of such jobs. As we have seen, a very high proportion of British women work part-time. However, market-led service expansion has also enabled women to move into higher-level jobs, as we have seen in Chapter 2.

France

The Esping-Andersen model would describe France as a 'corporatist' welfare state, based upon social insurance principles. However, unlike Germany (his major 'corporatist' example), a relatively high proportion of women in France are in employment, and women make up 42 per cent of the labour force. As Lewis (1992) and others have argued, the French state has recognized women as workers as well as mothers. As we shall see below, it has been argued that this is a consequence of the particular pronatalist policies which the French state developed in order to encourage women to bear and rear healthy children, and the way in which the state has organized support for families. These policies have made it easier for women in France to work full-time.

Norway

One might describe Norway as a social democratic or Scandinavian welfare state, developed after the Second World War. The contours of women's employment in Norway do indeed correspond to the Esping-Andersen model. Women massively predominate in welfare-state service employment, in the higher-level positions as well as the lower

(Kolberg and Kolstad 1993). However, the level of state-provided childcare in Norway is below that of the other Scandinavian welfare states (Leira 1992), although it is increasing.

Czech Republic

In the ex-state-socialist countries, welfare benefits were provided on a universal basis, and there was no market or private sector which sold them. Women were encouraged to enter the labour force—indeed, paid work was regarded as a national duty. However, although benefits were universal, the state socialist system was plagued by inadequacies—of housing, supplies of consumer goods, and so on. Thus it was widely supplemented by a system of 'self-welfare', focused upon women-centred family networks. Thus women's unpaid caring role in the household did not disappear under state socialism.

In summary

In Norway and Britain, the broad contours of women's employment correspond to what might have been predicted by Esping-Andersen's model: relatively high levels of employment for women in both countries, a very heavy concentration of women in the state-welfare sector in Norway, more polarization (that is, job inequality) and private-sector women's jobs in Britain. The structure of French women's employment does not correspond to the Esping-Anderson model of the 'corporatist' welfare state, and further explanations must be looked for. In the case of the Czech Republic, it seems to be the case that ideological considerations were the major determinants of women's employment levels.

The 'Equality Agenda'

As described above, the 'equality agenda' is being used here as a short-hand description of the aim of achieving equality between members of a nation state, which would include gender equality. In general, liberal democracies have focused largely upon an equality of rights or condition and thus the removal of legal and other restrictions on women, such as attaining the franchise, equal opportunities in education, access to employment, and so on. In relation to the market, men and women should be treated the same. Equal opportunity to compete does not necessarily result in an equal outcome, but this is not seen as a problem if everybody has equal rights in the beginning. Governments in *Britain* have largely restricted themselves to this liberal version of the equality agenda. For example, the government has passed equal-opportunities legislation and outlawed discrimination against women, but it has never considered 'affirmative action'—that is, special treatment for women or minorities to help them 'catch up'.

However, other countries have developed rather different versions of the 'equality agenda' for women. In the *Czech Republic*,[4] 'state social-ism' was associated with an equality agenda which privileged work in the public sphere—that is, employment (Scott 1974). Following Engels' (1940) influential arguments, paid employment was seen as the major avenue through which women's equality should be achieved. State so-cialism gave women equal rights in education, to enter the professions, and so on. The demands of women's market work have been re-cognized in the state's provision of childcare for working mothers, but domestic work, and the division of labour in the household, was, ideologically, not seen as particularly important—although from the 1960s, the 'double burden' of state socialist women was increasingly recognized.

In contrast to the Soviet-bloc countries, Scandinavian social demo-cratic socialism has, under the influence of 'second-wave' feminism, also recognized the significance of caring work in the private sphere to the 'equality agenda', as well as equality in employment (Hernes 1987; Persson 1990). That is, it has been argued that moves towards equality have to include changing the gender division of labour in the domestic sphere. The state offers help to parents in caring, particularly for chil-dren. Two broad strategies have been associated with the recognition of the value of caring in Scandinavian socialism: that of compensating the carer (who can be either male or female) for loss of earnings associated with childcare (through such strategies as maternity/paternity leaves and leaves for children's illness); and/or that of providing childcare so that carers may remain in employment. *Norway*, our Scandinavian ex-ample, is characterized by very generous maternity and paternity leaves (a proportion of childcare leave must be taken by the father), together with caring allowances, but the level of state-provided childcare is rela-tively low, although on the increase (Leira 1992; 1994).

France is unusual in that legal, constitutional equality for women has not had a high profile—the opposite, in fact, of the situation in Britain. French women were not given the vote until after the Second World War, and until 1965 French men were legally able to prevent their wives from working (Lewis 1992).[5] Paradoxically, however, economic support for the family in France has strengthened women's position in the labour market, as we shall see.

In summary, Britain has pursued a liberal version of the equality agenda. Women have been given formal, equal rights with men, and discrimination has been made illegal. However, the British state has not gone out of its way to give any special help to women as workers. In the Czech Republic, the state-socialist version of the equality agenda was fulfilled by moving women into employment—although working mothers were given help, state-socialist ideology paid no attention to gender relations in the private or domestic sphere, or to women's unpaid labour. Norway has followed an equality agenda influenced by 'second-wave' feminism, and thus in working towards equality, the unpaid domestic work of caring has been taken into account as well as paid employment. Until recently France has not given much attention to formal gender equality, and indeed, domestic patriarchy was legally maintained until the 1960s.

The State's Role in Supporting Mothers

Most nation states have recognized the value of motherhood as part of a strategy to persuade women to reproduce more citizens. To varying extents, nation states have been concerned about the reproduction and replacement of their populations, and have engaged in pronatalist policies—that is, persuading women of their national duty to bear and rear healthy children.

Two rather different strategies may be used by the state to try to ensure the reproduction of healthy infants. First, the state may attempt to keep women in the home, by co-operating in strategies which exclude them from paid work. On the other hand, the state may offer support to women to make it less difficult for them to work, and thus better able to care for their children. Clearly, the kind of policy followed by the state in these matters will have an important impact on the structure of women's employment.

In *Britain* experts in public health argued that the health of infants was to be best achieved by ensuring maternal care. From the nineteenth century onwards, public health efforts were focused upon, first, keeping mothers in the home, and second, educating them in hygiene and childcare (Lewis 1980; Jenson 1986). The British state opposed paid maternity leaves, and 'even in the inter-war years, never ratified the International Labour Organization's . . . provision for (paid maternity leave) . . . As one policy maker argued then, such provisions would be

wrong because they would usurp the father's responsibility for supporting the family and thus encourage family disintegration' (Jenson 1986:
21). Women were excluded from the labour market and 'women's
place' was firmly assigned to the home, where it was assumed that she
would be supported by her husband. Thus, historically, the British state
has always been extremely reluctant to provide any assistance with
childcare or other supports for working mothers, except in the special
conditions of the Second World War (Lewis 1992).

The formal barriers to women's labour-force participation in Britain
have been gradually removed, but the state has done little actively to
facilitate women's participation in the labour force through help with
childcare. The extent of public childcare provision in Britain is the lowest in Europe (Phillips and Moss 1988). Even when the British government has recognized the childcare needs of working mothers, it has
argued that these needs should be met by the employers, rather than
the state (Cmnd.1988). So whilst women in Britain are not now discouraged from becoming workers—indeed, at times of actual or potential
labour shortage they have been actively encouraged to join the labour
force—working mothers or other women with caring and domestic responsibilities are expected to make their own arrangements for caring.
In the 1990s the net result is that, 'Working parents (in Britain) with
children under 3 must rely almost entirely on either the private market
or their social networks' (Moss 1991: 125) for childcare.

In contrast, in *France*, the other strategy to encourage women to bear
and look after children—that is, making it easier to combine home and
work—has been followed. Indeed, the state's policy in respect of
women and the family has modified considerably Esping-Anderson's
'corporatist' welfare-state model as far as the structure and extent of
women's employment in France is concerned (Lane 1993). Policy-
makers in France concerned with infant welfare in the nineteenth century argued that the major problem was a too-early return to work by
mothers (Jenson 1986); thus, paid maternity leave in France was introduced in 1913. There have been no systematic attempts by the state to
push women out of the labour market in France. Lewis (1992) suggests
that this was because patriarchal control was located within the family.
French husbands could prevent their wives going out to work, or open-
ing bank accounts, until 1965 (although there is little evidence that
many did so). French governments have a long history of pronatalism,
but the strategy that has been followed has been to give generous child
benefits in order to compensate parents for the costs of having children,
and/or to make it easier for women to have children and carry on

working. European comparisons place France amongst the countries providing the highest level of publicly provided childcare. Nearly all French children between the ages of 3 and 6 (94 per cent) and a fair proportion of 2-year-olds attend nursery school which is free and provided by the state (Le Prince 1991). There is state provision for under threes in full-time *crèches collectives*, tax relief on childcare expenses, and, in addition, an *allocation de garde d'enfant à domicile* may be paid to working mothers towards the cost of care of children under three (Hantrais 1993).

Pronatalism in France has led to family policies which have redistributed income towards families and households with dependent children. Under the Family Code of 1939, benefits to families have been funded by employers' contributions. Since the 1970s benefits have been collected together in the *Complement Familiale* which, although means-tested to a certain extent, is paid whether or not the mother is in employment—which will greatly increase the likelihood of employment amongst single mothers. In general, Lewis (1992) has argued that French policy has been adapted so as to fit to the reality of changes in women's labour-market behaviour, and the contemporary argument is that women should be given a choice between childcare and paid work. In contrast, as we have seen, the British state has offered hardly anything by way of practical assistance.

Czechoslovakia, like France, has a recent history of active pronatalism, particularly during the period of state socialism. In the 1960s, there was increasing concern at the declining birthrate. Concerns about the reproduction, even replacement, of the population (during the state-socialist era, it was not possible to make up deficiencies in population levels through immigration) led governments to begin to recognize the particular needs of women, which had been largely ignored in ideologies dominated by the image of the 'worker'. In 1971 a generous system of paid maternity leave was introduced (now extending to three years), together with other inducements, such as access to housing (only couples with a child had any chance at all of acquiring accommodation), and other benefits, such as marriage loans for couples with deductions from repayments following the birth of the first child (Mozny 1993). However, the level of state-provided childcare in Czechoslovakia was somewhat lower than in other state-socialist countries (Heitlinger 1979). Nevertheless, as in France, pronatalist policies did give active support to motherhood, making paid employment for mothers somewhat easier. However, the distribution difficulties associated with state socialism, and the parallel developments in 'self-welfare', locked Czech women firmly into extended caring roles and the domestic sphere. The relatively young retirement ages (55 for women) meant that grandmothers on a pension were available for childcare whilst the mother earned the essential second income and related benefits.

In both France and the Czech Republic, therefore, support for mothers and thus help with caring has been provided by the state largely as part of policies to persuade women to have more children: they have been directed at women as mothers, rather than women as workers. In *Norway*, however, state assistance with caring has been developed as part of the state's efforts to achieve equality for women with men, a policy which was also implemented in other Scandinavian countries (Persson 1990). There are differences between the Scandinavain countries in the strategies developed to achieve equality for women (Leira 1994), and arguments about which system of support best suits women's interests. Nevertheless, women's equality is a major and explicit policy objective. Although the figure is low in comparison to other Scandinavian countries, nevertheless 55 per cent of age 3 to school-age children have places in publicly funded childcare. In Norway, a feature of the debate around 'women's work' was that, to some extent, domestic caring be recognized as 'work'. Pension schemes are maintained (admittedly at a rather low level) for women taking childrearing breaks, and both parents are entitled to leave to care for sick children.

In summary, there are considerable differences in policies towards women, as workers and as mothers, in the four nation states under discussion here. Britain may be described as a liberal welfare state, and it has also pursued liberal policies in relation to gender equality in employment. Thus there are today few restrictions on the behaviour of individuals, but the state has not actively intervened to support women's equality in employment, by providing childcare, for example. France has been less concerned with formal, legal equality for women, but has not sought to exclude women from employment and, as part of its programme of pronatalism and assistance to families, has given extensive assistance with childcare. The Czech Republic has positively encouraged employment for women in promoting women's equality. Since the 1960s, pronatalism has also resulted in some recognition of women's caring role but, as was usual in the state-socialist countries, few efforts have been made to generate equality in the domestic sphere. In contrast, in Norway, equality for women has been seen to require not only equality in employment, but also the recognition of women's caring work and changes in the domestic sphere.

Women's Employment Patterns

How are these cross-national differences reflected in women's employment? Women make up a similar proportion of the labour force in all four countries (Table 3.1). The broad contours of occupational segregation by sex are also very similar. Women predominate in service work, in particular health, and education, rather than manufacturing. The importance of these cross-national continuities in women's caring work, in both paid employment as well as in the domestic sphere, should not be under-estimated. However, as suggested in Chapter 2, it may be argued that the fact that men and women do different jobs is not such a matter of concern if this difference is not reflected in material inequalities (that is, vertical segregation) between men and women—and thus women's dependence.

Table 3.1 records differences in hourly wage rates between men and women in manual manufacturing work in the different countries. This indicator is not ideal, but it is important to make standardized comparisons. It can be seen that, in comparison to men, women have achieved the greatest level of equality in Norway. Norway has pursued an explicit equality agenda for women, informed by the arguments of second-wave feminism and giving explicit recognition to the value of caring work. Perhaps we should not be surprised, in these circumstances, that Norwegian women have done rather well. However, even though explicit equality policies have not been followed in France, French women's hourly rates are nearly 80 per cent of men's. Women in the Czech

Table 3.1 Employment, male/female wage differentials, and part-time work

% female-to-male hourly rates (manual workers, manufacturing):	Norway	France	Czech Republic	UK
1975	78.0	76.4	n/a	66.5
1987	83.7	79.5	n/a	68.0
1991–2	87.0	79.0	75.0	68.0
(*Source*: ILO)				
Part-time work (women, %): (*Source*: OECD; Czech statistics)	47.1	24.5	9.5	44.6
Women as a percentage of the labour force:	46	43	47	43

Republic do nearly as well as French women, and British women do least well of all in relation to men.

It might be argued that these differences in hourly wage-rates between women in the four countries are a reflection of other differences in the structure of women's employment in the four countries. For example, as we have already noted in this chapter, there are considerable differences in the extent of part-time work between women in different countries. In general, part-time work amongst women tends to bring down their wage levels, as we have seen in Chapter 2 (Rubery *et al.* 1994). Table 3.1 shows that there are, in fact, very substantial differences between the four countries in levels of part-time work—from under 10 per cent in the Czech Republic to 47 per cent in Norway. However, the countries with the 'best' and 'worst' hourly wage rates (Norway and the UK) had similar levels of part-time employment (Table 3.1).[6]

The UK has a high rate of part-time work amongst women. However, as we have seen in Chapter 2, part-time work in the UK is of poor quality. Employees working less than sixteen hours a week require five years' continuous service before they are entitled to employment protection (none at all for those working less than eight hours), and no National Insurance is payable for those earning less than £56 per week. The British government has systematically resisted attempts to implement EU directives to give part-time workers greater protection, although this is changing. As a consequence, British employers have had a virtually free hand as far as part-time workers are concerned. This has had a tendency to depress hourly wage rates amongst part-timers. For example, New Earnings Survey data shows that part-time hourly rates amongst women in UK manufacturing are 81 per cent of full-time hourly rates. Thus a combination of a liberal welfare state, giving no assistance with childcare, and a low level of labour-market regulation has been negative for British women. Britain has the highest levels of part-time working amongst mothers of young children, on the lowest rates of pay.

The level of part-time work amongst women is lower in France. Part-time work is more frequently found amongst younger (childless) women, where it is seen as a strategy for integrating women into the labour force if full-time work is not available. The notion of *temps choisi* has been developed as a strategy of sharing out available work. In any case, part-time employment in France is more likely to be 'good' part-time work, with longer hours, and with rates and conditions of employment protected by the corporatist deal. The *Code du Travail*, which was modified in 1981 to permit the development of part-time working, specifies that there should be no discrimination between full and part-time workers.

In Norway social rights are entirely independent of working-time thresholds, and part-timers are protected to the same extent as full-timers. Part-time work has undergone what Ellingsaeter (1992) has described as a 'normalization' process since the early 1980s: 'in general part-time workers work increasingly longer hours, have more secure work contracts and are often members of unions' (p. 32). Thus in Norway there are high levels of part-time work, but this work is highly protected by the welfare-state deal in which the availability of part-time work is seen as part of the package of choices offered to women in order to combine caring and market work.

In the UK, therefore, the combination of a liberal welfare-state regime together with an increasingly deregulated labour market have combined to give British women relatively poor work and low wage-rates. France and Norway have very different levels of part-time working amongst women. It may be suggested that the varying levels of state-provided childcare provision are important here. As we have seen, state-funded childcare for children in Norway is low by Scandinavian standards, and lags considerably behind that of France. Largely because of problems with childcare, many Norwegian women work part-time. However, part-time work in Norway is of high quality, and therefore the preponderance of part-time work amongst Norwegian women does not appear to have seriously affected wage-rates.

The Norwegian case demonstrates the potential of an active agenda of equality of outcome for women. It would seem that the emphasis given to the need to give material recognition to caring work, as second-wave feminism argued, has been very important here. In contrast, the Czech case suggests that the ex-state-socialist equality agenda was not very successful as far as *gender* equality was concerned, even though Czech pronatalism has resulted in the material recognition of childcare. This argument, of course, is neither new nor uncontroversial, as it has long been recognized that the double burden of women under state socialism played the major part in the persisting disadvantage of women during the state socialist era. However, it may be suggested that the case of France serves to reinforce further the point that the equality agenda should incorporate the material recognition of *caring* work, as well as a formal equality of such matters as employment rights. On average, women in France have fared better in material terms (in respect of employment) than women in Britain and in the Czech republic. The weight of evidence suggests that the extent and nature of childcare provision has been crucial here, even though it has not been introduced as part of an equality agenda.

Summary and Conclusions

In this chapter we have moved beyond the British case in order to better understand the factors structuring women's employment patterns. State policies in a wide range of areas—welfare policy, reproducing the national population, the nation's health, and equality amongst its citizens—will all have an impact on women's labour-force participation. As we have seen, these policies are very different in different countries; therefore, we would anticipate that there will be differences in women's employment patterns as well. Support for mothers would seem to be particularly important: as we have seen, formal equality for women as such did not achieve a high profile in France, but assistance to women as mothers has apparently resulted in greater equality for French women, in comparison to British women, in employment.

Although this book is mainly concerned with women's employment in Britain, this chapter has shown that we should be careful not to generalize from the British case to women's employment as a whole. Walby has identified the British state as playing a major role in the institution of 'public patriarchy'. However, in Scandinavia the state has been seen as 'woman-friendly' (Hernes 1987), with the capacity to bring in policies which level patriarchal inequalities. High levels of part-time work in Britain no doubt reflect the goverment's promotion of labour-market 'flexibility', but as far as women are concerned, the low availability of childcare in Britain must also be an important factor. As we saw in Chapter 2, the majority of female part-time workers say that they prefer to work part-time, but this preference has to be evaluated against the necessity to arrange for private childcare. In any case, we also saw in Chapter 2 that, even if British women valued the convenient hours of part-time work, they were also aware of its disadvantages. The example of Norway suggests that part-time work need not necessarily also be disadvantaged employment.

In summary, this chapter has demonstrated that:

- There are important cross-national continuities in the structuring of women's employment. The increase in service jobs, often associated with welfare state expansion, has created many new jobs for women, and women predominate in 'caring' occupations. Thus there are many parallels in the broad patterns of occupational segregation between different countries.

- Nevertheless, there are also significant differences—in levels of part-time work, and in levels of women's material reward compared to men. These reflect specific historical developments and demonstrate the significance of national context (and therefore structural factors) in shaping women's employment patterns. For example, it is easier for women in France to 'choose' to work full-time, whereas Czech women had little 'choice' about whether or not to work during the era of state socialism.

- More generally, our discussion has also further demonstrated the importance of taking into account non-market or caring work in any discussion of women's paid employment.

In Chapter 4, therefore, we will explore in greater depth the employment/family interface amongst women in Britain.

Chapter Four

Women's Employment and the Family

Introduction

One of the central themes of this book has been an emphasis upon the reciprocal relationship between paid and unpaid, market and non-market work. Thus changes in women's participation in market work will obviously have an impact on non-market work, which is usually carried out in the domestic or 'private' sphere. In this chapter, therefore, we will examine the changes in family formation and family building which have run in parallel with changes in women's paid employment, and their consequences for both the meshing of employment with family life. We will also be discussing changes in relationships within the household itself, and some of the wider implications of these changes for the structure of social inequality in Britain.

Some sociologists—notably Giddens (1992) and Beck (1992)—have suggested that one important result of the changes in the status of women, including the rise in women's employment, is that household and personal relationships are having to be renegotiated as well. The 'male-breadwinner' model of the division of labour was associated with a model of family life described by the term 'nuclear' or 'conjugal' family, in which the stereotypical household would include a male partner, a non-working female partner, and their dependent children. Women's paid employment immediately changes this model. In the nuclear family, women are economically dependent upon their male supporter. Economic dependence is reflected in their subordinate position within the household. 'Women's liberation' and rising female employment has meant that an increasing number of women have rejected their subordinate roles and positions in relation to men. Besides documenting the changes that have taken place in family and household building, therefore, we will also examine evidence describing some of the ways in which people have adapted (or not) to the changing circumstances of the gender division of labour.

One of the most striking trends affecting families and households has been the decline in fertility, that is, in the average number of children born to women. Fertility rates have been going down over the whole of Europe. The total period fertility rate in the UK (that is, the average number of children that would be born to each woman if the current birth-rates remained the same throughout her child-bearing life) peaked at 2.95 in 1964, then fell rapidly to a low point of 1.69 in 1977 (all figures in the section are taken from *Social Trends 1996*). In 1994 it was 1.75, which was still well below the rate of 2.1 which would be required for long-term population replacement. Women, therefore, are having fewer children, and it is unlikely that this trend will be reversed. Many women are also deferring childbearing, and the average age at

Fig. 4.1 Marriages and divorces in the UK since 1961

United Kingdom

Thousands

[a] Including annulments
[b] For one or both partners
Source: Office of Population Censuses and Surveys; General Register Office (Scotland); General Register Office (Northern Ireland)

which women have their first child has been rising. Although women aged 25 to 29 are still the most likely to give birth, since 1992 women in their early thirties have been more likely to have a baby than women in their early twenties, and over a third of women born in 1962 were still childless at 30.

The number of people getting married has fallen, and the number of divorces has risen. Indeed, Britain has the highest divorce rate in Europe at the moment (the divorce rate has fallen in other countries, such as Denmark, which once had a higher divorce rate). The average age of first-time marriage has been rising, and now stands at 28 for men and 26 for women.

On average, therefore, people are marrying later, having their children later, and are more likely to suffer a marriage break-up. The proportion of births outside marriage has also been increasing—from under 10 per cent in the 1970s to over 30 per cent in 1994. The majority of such births occur within stable relationships, and the proportion of births outside marriage which were jointly registered has increased from three-fifths in 1981 to nearly four-fifths in 1993. Nevertheless, this trend, together with the increase in marriage breakdown, means that an increasing number of children are living with only one parent. The proportion of dependent children living in one-parent families has tripled since 1972; and 19 per cent of children lived with just their mother and 1 per cent with just their father in 1994–5. Smaller families, the greater likelihood of marriage break-up and lone parenthood, together with an ageing population, have resulted in a decreasing size of household and an increasing proportion of one-person households. Indeed, households containing a stereotypical 'family' of two parents and dependent children now make up only 25 per cent of the total.

The Family–Employment Interface: Working Mothers

In Chapter 2, we already saw that women's employment levels have been rising whilst men's have been in decline. Amongst women, it is employment amongst mothers that has been rising the most rapidly. Between 1984 and 1994 the economic activity rate for mothers (that is, women with dependent children under 16) increased from 55 per cent to 64 per cent, compared with an increase from 66 per cent to 71 per cent for all working women (all figures in this section are taken from Sly 1994). Indeed, the greatest increase in labour-market participation since 1984 has been amongst women with children under 5; from 37 per cent in 1984 to 52 per cent in 1993/4. The proportion of women in employment goes up as children get older, and over three-quarters of married women whose youngest child is aged between 11 and 15 are in employment. There has been a small decline in the number of women working full-time, reflecting the decline in the number of full-time jobs, so the recent increase in mothers' employment has been in part-time working.

The pattern of the increase in mothers' employment has been moulded to the contours of the existing structures of household inequality. Thus mothers in couples are more likely to be economically active (67 per cent) than lone mothers (48 per cent). Whereas half of all mothers in couple relationships with children under 5 are working, this is true of only a quarter of lone mothers with children of the same age. The unemployment rate of lone mothers is 20 per cent, as compared to only 7 to 8 per cent for mothers in couples. Lone-parent families (and we should remember that 20 per cent of all children live in lone-parent families) are much more likely to be families in which no-one is employed than are two-parent families. Both parents are unemployed in only 11 per cent of two-parent families with children under 16, but 61 per cent of lone mothers and 46 per cent of lone fathers are not in employment. A similar pattern of cumulative disadvantage, reflected in women's employment, is also to be found in couple families. Mothers whose husbands/partners are unemployed are less likely to be in employment (24 per cent) than are those with employed husbands (68 per cent).

Employment amongst mothers, therefore, is more likely to be found amongst women with partners or husbands than women who are lone parents, and amongst the wives of men who are employed rather than the wives of men who are unemployed. A similar pattern of inequality-reinforcing employment patterns amongst women is to be seen in the relative rates of mothers' employment by qualification level. In 1993/4, 82 per cent of mothers with higher (that is, above degree-level) qualifications were in employment, as compared to 65 per cent of mothers with qualifications at or below A level, and only 40 per cent of mothers with no qualifications.

Mothers, particularly mothers of young children, are, therefore, the fastest-growing section of the labour force. Within this group, however, employment is rising most rapidly of all amongst well-educated women living in a partnership (Harrop and Moss 1994). Thus the way in which the increase in mothers' employment has been distributed has contributed to growing polarization and social inequality in British society. We will be discussing the implications of this trend later in this chapter. First, however, we will examine the practical aspects of this rise in the employment of mothers. If mothers of children under 5 are, increasingly, going 'out to work', who is caring for their children?

In Chapter 3, we already saw that, in comparison with the rest of Europe, Britain has the lowest level of state-provided childcare. As we have seen, Moss has argued: 'Working parents (in Britain) with children under three must rely almost entirely on either the private market or their social networks' (1991: 125). Another way in which mothers combine paid work with childcare, as we saw in Chapter 2, is for mothers to work from home. Mothers of older children may be able to find work which takes place only during school hours, and of course, older children do not necessarily require permanently available care—maternal or otherwise. Table 4.1 summarizes the pattern of childcare arrangements amongst working mothers in Britain today. (More than one form of childcare may be used by working mothers, so the percentages in the table add up to more than 100).

It can be seen that by far the greater proportion of childcare relies on networks of families and friends (including partners), and may be described as 'informal'. The proportion of mothers paying for individual childminders or nannies is very small (indeed, only 2 per cent of all working mothers in the survey said that they employed nannies), and nearly a third of mothers avoided the cost of childcare by only working when children were at school, or by working from home. Childcare arrangements, however, will obviously vary considerably according to the age of the child. Table 4.2, therefore, gives details of childcare

---

Table 4.1 Childcare arrangements of all working women with dependent children, 1994 (multiple response, percentages)

Childminder or nanny	13
Nursery, crèche, nursery school, or playgroup	11
After-school or holiday playscheme	4
Partner	33
Parents/parents-in-law	32
Other relatives and friends	18
Children old enough to look after themselves	24
Only works when children are at school	22
Works at home	8
Number of mothers	3,438

Source: adapted from Finlayson, Ford, and Marsh (1996)

Table 4.2 Childcare arrangements of working mothers by age of their youngest child, 1994, percentages

Youngest child: age	0–4	5–10	11–15	16+	All
Professional only	24	10	2	—	12
Combination	23	10	3	—	11
Informal only	48	54	40	8	45
Child old enough	—	—	28	78	14
Avoid childcare	5	26	28	13	19
Numbers	1,016	950	896	213	3,087

Source: as Table 4.1

arrangements for children of different ages. 'Professional' childcare denotes childcare that is paid for—that is, childminders, nannies, nurseries, crèches, nursery school or playgroup; 'informal' childcare includes partners, parents, and friends, and double counting has been avoided by identifying mothers using a combination of professional and informal childcare separately. The 'avoid childcare' category includes mothers who only work school hours, or who work from home.

Table 4.2 shows that the use of paid childcare is heavily concentrated amongst mothers of children under school age—this group of mothers, it will be remembered, is the most rapidly expanding section of the labour force—but nevertheless, nearly half these mothers rely on childcare help from partners, parents, and friends. Paid childcare drops off steeply as children get older, as might be expected.

Surveys of childcare arrangements similar to that used in Tables 4.1 and 4.2 were also carried out in 1991 and 1992, so some idea of recent trends can be given. The proportion of mothers using any professional childcare has risen from 20 per cent to 23 per cent, reflecting the increase in employment of mothers with young children, the group most likely to use paid childcare. The costs of childcare have also risen, from a mean of 110p per hour worked by the mother in 1991, to 154p per hour worked in 1994. Employment amongst mothers of young children might be rising, therefore, but these figures suggest that mothers have to buy themselves back in to the labour market, and that the costs of this buy-back are on the increase.

The increase in the level of paid childcare, of course, means that the numbers of paid workers (who are usually women) providing this childcare is increasing as well. As we saw in Chapter 3, the British government's policy has been to encourage the growth in the market for

Table 4.3 Domestic caring occupations

Standard occupational classification	Total	Men	Women
644 care assistants	28,276	1,705	26,571
650 nursery nurses	5,925	72	5,853
651 playgroup leaders	1,957	66	1,891
659 other childcare and related	19,211	196	19,015
670 domestic housekeepers	3,082	347	2,735
958 cleaners, domestics	77,860	11,784	66,076
Total%	100%	10%	90%

Source: 1991 census

private service provision, rather than to organize public provision of these services. Thus not only childcare, but a range of other caring services once provided within the household (that is, by women) are now a source of paid employment.

It is difficult to be precise about the numbers of people who are now employed to carry out work once done by women in the home. For example, one of the fastest-growing parts of the service sector in Britain is the 'hospitality industry'—hotels and catering. Although some of this work might be a substitute for home cooking, most of this expansion will reflect changing patterns of consumption. Table 4.3 gives details of more specifically domestic, 'caring' occupations.

It may be seen that, as might have been expected, caring jobs are overwhelmingly 'women's work'. Only 10 per cent of paid carers in these categories are men, and in some categories, such as childcare and work related to it, men form only 1 per cent of the total. The extent of this kind of paid work has been increasing in the recent past, but still only represents under 1 per cent of all paid jobs in Britain.

Only a minority of households, of course, will actually employ paid domestic workers, but this minority is on the increase given the growing proportion of well-qualified mothers who are returning to work whilst their children are young. Gregson and Lowe (1994) have estimated the pattern of increase in demand for paid domestic workers by analysing the advertisements for such jobs (in magazines such as *The Lady*). The advertised demand for such workers increased very rapidly—in fact, more than doubled—throughout the 1980s, but fell off with the onset of the economic recession in 1990. They found that the kinds of jobs advertised changed over the decade. In the early 1980s the demand for paid domestic labour was mainly for housekeepers and mothers' helps, whilst by the end of the 1980s the major category of demand was for nannies to care for young children, reflecting the increasing number of mothers of young children staying in work. Childcare is obviously very important, but in their interviews with employers of domestic labour Gregson and Lowe also found that, very often, working couples paid for domestic help in order to give them more 'quality time' with each other, as well as to resolve conflicts over who did the domestic work. It was the most unpopular tasks—in particular, household cleaning—which led to conflict, and it was men's refusal to clean (or rather, their inability to 'see' household dirt) which had led to the employment of a cleaner.

The wages of paid domestic workers are low. Actual pay levels for cleaning reported by Gregson and Lowe in the early 1990s (pp. 208–9) range from £2.50 to £4 an hour (usually 'cash in hand'). Many nannies live in, and may receive benefits 'in kind'; but even taking this into account, salaries are low. In the North-East, 88 per cent of nannies did not have a signed contract of employment. The average gross annual earnings of nannies in the families they studied were £4,800 in the North-East, and £7,200 in the South-East.

In this section of the chapter, then, we have focused upon recent trends in mother's employment and its consequences. We have seen that employment is rising fastest amongst mothers of young children, and that there has been a corresponding increase in the demand for childcare. Most childcare is arranged through informal sources—partners, families, or friends—or the mother adjusts her own paid work to accommodate childcare; but the level of professional (that is, paid) childcare has been increasing, as has its cost. In Britain, there is very little by way of publicly provided childcare, and families must make private arrangements, either paid or unpaid. Such employment is on the increase, but is largely unregulated and poorly paid. Gregson and Lowe suggest that as long as such caring is left to 'private' arrangements, this situation will persist.

As more women go 'out to work', therefore, caring work is becoming, increasingly, 'marketized'—that is, carried out for money rather than because of love, duty, or social obligation. We should be careful, however, not to over-estimate the extent to which this 'commodification of caring' is taking place. As we have seen, the most recent figures show that the care of children of employed mothers is still largely achieved either with help from family, friends, and partners, or through the mother making work arrangements which are sufficiently flexible to accommodate childcare. Nevertheless, to the extent that private-sector caring jobs are insecure and poorly paid, then the increase in their number will contribute further to the increase in social inequality which, as we have seen, has also been made worse by the pattern of the increase in women's employment and the growing polarization between 'work-rich' households, containing two people in paid employment, and 'work-poor' households, containing none (Joseph Rowntree Foundation 1995: 22).

Some people might want to argue that the consequences for society of the increasing employment of women have been largely negative. Birth-rates have gone down, divorce rates have risen, lone parenthood has increased, social inequalities at the level of the household have become greater, and the number of poorly paid jobs (sometimes called 'junk jobs') has risen. However, it would be mistaken to see rising levels of women's employment as having *caused* these phenomena. As we saw in Chapters 2 and 3, the underlying trend of women's employment rates has been upward in all societies. Smaller families, and increasing pressure from women for equality, mean that it is extremely unlikely that women would agree to be returned to the home and a lifetime of unpaid caring. However, the *circumstances* of the increase in women's employment are not randomly determined. Governments, in particular, play an important part in determining the context of this expansion, as we saw in Chapter 3.

In the British case, the Conservative government has removed or reduced important labour-market protections, such as wage protection for the lowest-paid workers (through the abolition of Wages Councils), and legislation to reduce the power of trade unions to protect their members; and, as we saw in Chapter 2, it has encouraged the development of the 'flexible' labour force—for example, by privatizing publicly provided services. As we have seen, where caring services are required (such as childcare and eldercare) and cannot be met by the family, then they must be met, however inadequately, in the market place. It may be argued, therefore, that deregulation and marketization have been the most important factors in encouraging the expansion of low-level jobs, rather than the increase of women's employment as such. This is not the case in all countries. As we have seen in Chapter 3, in the Scandinavian countries for example, the state's approach to caring and welfare provision created relatively 'good' jobs in the public sector.

Similarly, a lack of job availability—particularly of relatively secure, full-time jobs—will tend to discourage the formation of stable families. As Wilson (1993) has argued in his discussion of the 'underclass' in the United States (another society in which the labour market has been deregulated and there has been an expansion of 'junk jobs'), one of the major factors contributing to the increase in the proportion of lone mothers has been the decline in suitable permanent partners for mothers. As the number of low-level, relatively unskilled jobs available declines, so men not in employment find it increasingly difficult, if not impossible, to set up families.

In short, an increase in competition, which in Britain has been a deliberate government policy, produces both winners and losers. There is a further tendency for winners to cluster together. Well-educated, job-marketable women are likely to enter into partnerships with similar men, and this will increase the extent of social inequality in an unregulated market. Families and households adjust to the circumstances in which they find themselves, but holding families together has become increasingly difficult for those who have lost out in the marketization of British society. It would be very misleading, therefore, to lay the blame for rising inequality in Britain on the increase in women's employment (we will be examining these arguments at greater length in Chapter 6).

In the first sections of this chapter, we have examined the changes in family formation which have accompanied the growth of women's employment, in particular the consequences of the increasing employment of mothers and the 'commodification of caring'. What, however, have been the consequences of these changes for relationships *within* the household? In the rest of this chapter we will examine recent research which has studied the impact of women's employment on family life.

The Domestic Division of Labour

The traditional male-breadwinner model of the gender division of labour, as we saw in Chapter 1, assumed that women were responsible for domestic work whilst men were responsible for market work. In one sense, therefore, in the 'pure' male-breadwinner model there was no gender division of labour in the home—the women did the work. With the increase in women's employment, however, the rationale for this broad division is undermined. If, increasingly, women engage in work outside the household, it might be argued, then men's work within the household should increase correspondingly—that is, men should increase their share of domestic work.

In the 1960s and 1970s, it was assumed by some sociologists that the rise in the number of working wives would indeed be accompanied by a corresponding increase in the husband's input into domestic work. For example, in their book *The Symmetrical Family* (1973), Young and Willmott argued that the middle classes in particular were leading the trend towards more egalitarian, 'symmetrical' marriage relationships in which husband and wife shared the tasks of both wage-earning and domestic labour. Their work was much influenced by the research of Elizabeth Bott (1957), who in an influential study had identified variations in the degree of 'jointness' and segregation' in husband's and wives' domestic and leisure activities. Bott distinguished between marriages embedded in 'close-knit' and 'loose-knit' family and neighbourhood networks. Husbands and wives whose networks were loose-knit were more likely to share in joint, rather than segregated, domestic and leisure activities. The development of Bott's work added a class dimension, in that close-knit networks were more likely to be found amongst working-class couples. Loose-knit networks, and more companionate domestic relations, were more likely to be found amongst the middle classes. Young and Wilmott's predictions of increasing domestic egalitarianism, therefore, have to be seen against the background of the broader debates that were taking place within the sociology of the 1960s—in particular, arguments that British society was becoming increasingly 'middle class' (see Goldthorpe *et al.* 1969).

However, empirical studies of the actual domestic division of labour between men and women suggested that this early optimism was unjustified. From the end of the 1970s in Britain, there was a period of economic recession and restructuring which was accompanied by rapidly rising male unemployment. However, studies of the household showed that men's loss of market work did not result in an increase in the amount of domestic labour they carried out. Indeed, for men who felt they had lost masculinity with the loss of their job, domestic work, which was identified as 'women's work', was something to be avoided (Morris 1990).

A period of rapidly rising male unemployment presents special problems. In practice, there is much variability in the extent to which men carry out domestic work, depending upon both the stage in the family life-cycle and social background more generally, as well as the amount of paid work carried out by the female partner. Mothers of young children, in particular, carry out very high levels of domestic work, and at this stage in the family life-cycle men often work long hours of market work in order to support the family. Men do more domestic work in the later stage of the family life-cycle, when women are more likely to be in employment (Pahl 1984). However, the extent to which the husband of a working wife carries out domestic work depends crucially upon whether the wife works full-time or part-time. As we can see from the data summarized in Figures 4.2 onwards, research shows that the gender division of domestic labour in households where the woman works part-time is not very different from households where the woman is not in employment. It is *full-time* employment that makes a difference. It is also apparent that, with the exception of small household repairs, women do more domestic work than men.

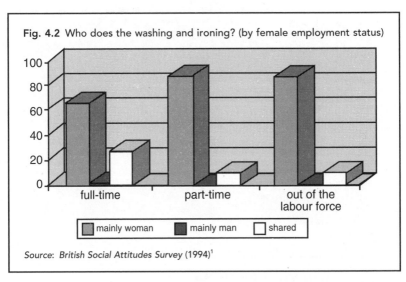

Fig. 4.2 Who does the washing and ironing? (by female employment status)

☐ mainly woman   ☐ mainly man   ☐ shared

Source: British Social Attitudes Survey (1994)[1]

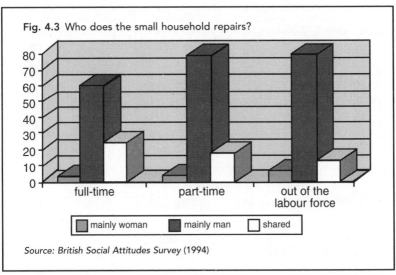

Fig. 4.3 Who does the small household repairs?

☐ mainly woman   ☐ mainly man   ☐ shared

Source: British Social Attitudes Survey (1994)

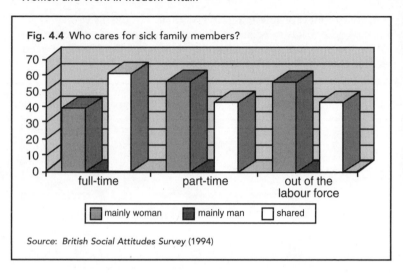

Fig. 4.4 Who cares for sick family members?

Source: *British Social Attitudes Survey* (1994)

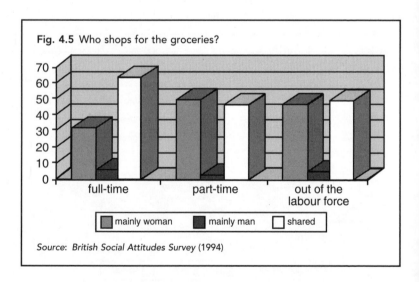

Fig. 4.5 Who shops for the groceries?

Source: *British Social Attitudes Survey* (1994)

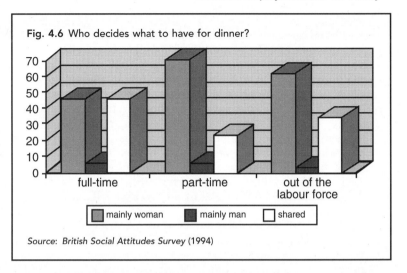

Fig. 4.6 Who decides what to have for dinner?

mainly woman ◼ mainly man ☐ shared

Source: *British Social Attitudes Survey* (1994)

Social background also has some effect—for example, Pahl (1984) found that the higher the wives' job status, the more domestic work done by the husband. Couples from higher social classes are also more likely to have egalitarian attitudes to gender and gender roles, although equality ideals may be frustrated by the demands of the husband's job (Morris 1990: 101; see also Gregson and Lowe 1994, discussed in the previous section).

A number of studies, therefore, have demonstrated that, although men do take on more domestic work as a consequence of their female partner's paid employment, nevertheless this increase does not equalize the amount of work carried out by men and women. In her review, Morris (1990) concludes that 'none of the data seems to warrant any suggestion that the traditional female responsibility for household work has been substantially eroded, or that male participation has substantially increased' (p. 102). Hochschild (1990) has described this as the 'stalled revolution'. Although, increasingly, women have moved into the previously male-dominated sphere of paid work, there has been no equivalent increase in the amount of unpaid work carried out by men—hence the gender revolution has been 'stalled': 'women have gone to work, but the workplace, the culture, and most of all, the men, have not adjusted themselves to the new reality'. Thus many women work a 'second shift', of household work as well as paid work.

However, Hakim (1996) suggests that much domestic labour is not strictly necessary, and should thought of as 'consumption', carried out for pleasure, rather than 'work'. She claims that this explains the fact that full-time housewives spend longer hours in domestic work than women in employment. Of course, much 'work', such as cooking, gardening, teaching, even writing books, is pleasurable, and people will spend longer doing it than is strictly required; but this does not mean that it is not 'work'.[2] Nevertheless, Hakim suggests that husbands are reluctant to help full-time housewives because they are inefficient (1996: 48). This suggestion not only assumes that any man's definition of household efficiency is superior to any woman's, but also fails to explain why the husbands of part-time women employees do not do more to assist their (presumably more efficient) wives. In any case, as Gregson and Lowe's research demonstrates, women in full-time employment are critical of their partner's domestic labour contribution.

Hakim also claims that the extent of women's caring work has been grossly over-estimated. Childcare, she says, is being compressed into a shorter time period, and men are as likely to be informal carers (for example, of the elderly) as women. These assertions raise large questions that cannot be properly discussed here. It might be suggested that, as adult children continue to live at home for longer periods, the period of caring involvement with children is actually going up rather than down. In any case, Hakim is not correct as far as participation in informal care is concerned. Mid-life women are particularly likely to be informal carers. Of women aged 45 to 60, 6 per cent provide care for someone in their household and 22 per cent for someone in another household, whereas the comparable proportions for men are 5 and 15 per cent (Arber and Ginn 1995: 452).

Nevertheless, changes are taking place, albeit very slowly, as is suggested by the fact that 15 per cent of middle-aged men do have caring responsibilities. Work on time budgets (Gershuny *et al.* 1994) suggests that inequalities in working hours between husbands and wives have decreased, but this is largely because women in employment have reduced their hours of housework, rather than that men have increased theirs. Warde and Hetherington's (1993) Manchester-based survey found that the gender stereotyping of domestic tasks remains very strong:

A wife was about 14 times more likely than her husband to have last done the ironing, almost 30 times as likely the washing, 9 times the tidying up, 7 times the cooking, twice the washing up. A husband was 4 times as likely to have done the painting or car washing, 20 times the plastering, 3 times cutting the lawn. (p. 32)

They conclude that men's domestic labour contribution is largely inflexible, and that men do female-ascribed, routine domestic tasks only when their partners are not around to do this work. However, their work also indicated the possibilities of change. Their study showed that, when household tasks were carried out by young people, gender stereotyping was less likely—there was less inequality in the younger generation. They also showed that men were considerably more likely than women to think that they did less than their fair share of housework. This suggests a change of attitude amongst men, in that it is no longer automatically assumed that housework *ought* to be a 'woman's' job.

Although, therefore, surveys of the domestic division of labour in households continue to show that women still carry a 'dual burden' of paid and domestic work, there are a number of indications of possible change. Gershuny and his colleagues (1994) argue that, over an extended period, the division of domestic labour is adapting to changing

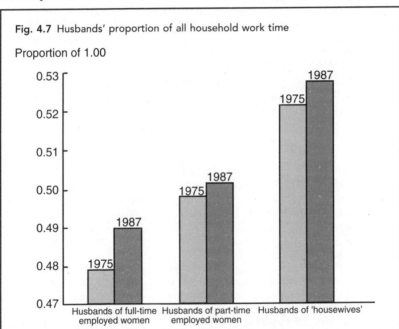

Fig. 4.7 Husbands' proportion of all household work time

Proportion of 1.00

Note: Because women still do more domestic work, husbands of women in full-time work do proportionately *less* total 'household work time' overall (i.e. paid and unpaid work, men and women) than those of women not in paid work. However, Fig. 4.7 indicates that men are increasing their proportion of total 'household work time' by doing more domestic (unpaid) work.
Source: Gershuny, Godwin, and Jones (1994)

circumstances, a process they describe as 'lagged adaptation'. Many of the people who are having to adjust to the realities of women's paid employment themselves grew up and were socialized at a time when the division of labour in the household was more likely to be conventional, and norms acquired in childhood take time to change. This does not mean, however, that nothing is happening.

Gershuny *et al.*'s data (the results of a survey of households carried out in 1987) showed that the division of household tasks remains conventional. As we have seen, women predominantly carry out cooking, cleaning, and clothes washing, men do jobs such as car maintenance. They also found, as with previous studies, that women with young children did most by way of domestic work, and that men only did significantly more domestic work when their wives worked full-time. Non-employed wives with full-time husbands did approximately 83 per cent of unpaid household work, as compared to 82 per cent of part-time employed wives; but full-time employed wives of full-time employed husbands do 73 per cent—and the longer the wife has been in employment, the more domestic work the husband is likely to do.

Whether or not a woman works full-time, therefore, is clearly important. However, the research also found that those couples who had parents with a relatively more egalitarian domestic division of labour were more likely to have a relatively egalitarian domestic division of labour themselves, suggesting that changes were taking place over time. They therefore compared the results of the 1987 survey with a similar survey carried out in 1975. This comparison showed that, in all household employment combinations (that is, whether the woman was not in employment, working full-time, or working part-time), the contribution of the husband to domestic work had increased. International comparisons also confirmed this general social trend. Gershuny *et al.* conclude, therefore:

With women's increasing entry into paid employment, so their total workload increases. . . . But the increase is moderated, though not entirely offset, by the substitution of some male unpaid work for some female. The compensation is not complete, the women's paid work increases faster than the men's substitution of unpaid for paid work, but nevertheless a process of adaptation is clearly under way. (pp. 184–5)

Changes in the gender division of market work, that is, women's entry into paid employment, have been achieved much more rapidly than changes in the gender division of non-market work (domestic labour). The most recent work suggests that a slow process of adaptation is under way, although it is likely that some gender stereotyping of household tasks will persist, as will the greater identification of women with the home in general. What, however, of the relationships between men and women? How is the greater participation of women in market work reflected in the way in which household affairs are organized? In the next section we will examine one important area: the control and management of money within the household.

Money and the Household

Much writing about 'the household' tends to assume, albeit implicitly, that all of the members of the household share the same interests. The idea of a 'household strategy', for example, treats the household as a single unit. However, as many authors have pointed out, this leaves out of account questions such as: Exactly *who* determines household strategies? Are the interests of some members of the household given priority over others? These questions are answered by what is described as the *resource theory* of power within the household (Morris 1990). In brief, this theory suggests that the person(s) with the greater power within the household are those who make the largest contribution to the resources of the unit. Thus it will usually be men, as the 'main breadwinners', who have the most power. If this theory holds good, then as women's material contribution to the household increases their relative power should be on the increase too.

However, historically, in Britain, even women who brought considerable property to a marriage had no control over it. Until the late nineteenth century a woman's property passed into the hands of the husband on marriage; similarly, any money a wife might earn or inherit during her marriage became her husband's property. Under common law, marriage meant that husband and wife became one person, and as Hartmann (1981) has remarked, this person was the man. Amongst the wealthy classes, equity law was developed which enabled property to be held in trust for women (and therefore safe from unsuitable husbands), but these trusts were controlled by male relatives. However, the absolute right of most men to their wives' property and earnings led to many cases of injustice, such as these which achieved public attention in the 1850s:

A lady was deserted by her husband, who went off with another woman to Australia to seek his fortune in the gold fields. She opened a school in order to support herself, but her husband, having failed in his venture, returned to England and seized all her property.

A woman was cruelly treated by her husband, who was at last convicted by a court of assault on her. Meanwhile her father died, leaving her considerable property. But the husband was the legal owner and since he was a convicted felon the property was forfeited to the crown. (cited in Pahl 1989: 19)

Pressures for reform of the law were resisted by those who argued that to change it would go against both the Church's position on marriage, that husband and wife were one, as well as the 'natural' subordination of women within marriage. Nevertheless, after a long struggle the Married Women's Property Act of 1882 gave married women the same rights over property as men and unmarried women.

Since the late nineteenth century, therefore, women's rights in respect of money and property have been the same as those of men. However, as we have seen, the male-breadwinner model and men's dominance in the world of employment meant that, in practice, only a small minority of women owned independent property, and most were dependent on their husbands. Thus, in the great majority of cases, it would be (and still is) men who will bring the greater material resources to the household.

How are these resources managed? Responsibility for finances operates on a number of levels. Jan Pahl (1983) has argued that we should distinguish between *control, management,* and *budgeting.* Control is concerned with the way in which money is distributed and with decisions on areas and objects of expenditure. As the decision-maker, the controller has the most power. Management describes the processes through which control decisions are actually carried out, in particular in which areas of expenditure. Thus the manager answers to the controller, but still has access to the whole pool of resources. Budgeting involves the least discretion, being the process of spending within particular categories, and achieving the most economical consumption requirements.

However, does the control of money necessarily equal power? Women in households with very low levels of income are very often in control of household budgets; but, in these cases, it is the activity of budgeting that will predominate, rather than control. In these circumstances control of household finance is more of a chore than a source of power. Research has shown that very low-income households are also likely to be characterized by very conventional attitudes to gender roles. Studies of middle-class couples suggest that although the partners may have more egalitarian attitudes, nevertheless it was the 'male providers' who made the major spending decisions. The situation is clearly very complex, and will be influenced by a range of factors including the total level of income within the household, the wife's employment status, social background, and the relationship between the couple themselves.

The research of Pahl (1989) and others on the management of money within the household not only demonstrates this complexity, but also shows how the situation has changed as more women have entered employment. Five basic categories of household management are identified:

- The *whole wage* system, in which one partner is responsible for managing all household income, and responsible for all expenditures. The whole wage system can be either:
- The *female whole wage system*, in which wives have sole responsibility for managing all household finances. This system has been traditionally associated with low-income families, with a traditional division of household labour. The husband hands over his pay packet, minus his personal spending money. With the rise in unemployment, particularly amongst men with few skills and qualifications, the 'wage' is nowadays likely to be some form of state benefit. This system has been reported as resented by wives, as it gives them no personal spending money, and the husband may be reluctant to earn extra money if he knows that it will go into household finances.
- The *male whole wage system*, in which husbands have sole responsibility for managing household finances. Again, this system tends to be found in low income households and has been found particularly in studies of abused women.
- The *allowance* system. Here the main earner hands over a set amount for housekeeping (the 'housekeeping allowance') and keeps the remainder of the money for their (usually his) personal expenditure. This system was held to be typical amongst traditional higher-earning working-class households, as well as middle-class households with a single earner. Often, the wife might not even be aware of the full extent of her husband's earnings, and extra earnings, such as bonus payments or overtime, might be retained by the husband.

Both kinds of whole-wage system and the allowance system tend to be associated with segregated gender roles and a relatively traditional division of labour.

- In the *pooling* or *joint management* system, both partners have access to all household income, and financial responsibilities are in principle joint. This system is particularly associated with households in which wives are in employment, and tends to reflect a more egalitarian relationship, often with a joint bank account.

- In the *independent management* system, each partner has access to money which they personally control. Neither has access to all the household money, and each partner is responsible for particular items of household expenditure. It is a strategy of household management which may be adopted in order to avoid conflict, and may also be used by wives whose earnings in the main supplement an inadequate housekeeping allowance.

A common finding of earlier studies was that relatively more of a woman's earnings would be used on household expenditure, even if her paid job was seen as paying for 'extras'. In contrast, men's extra earnings were more likely to be seen as 'pocket money'. Many women with housekeeping allowances express a desire for a paid job so that they do not have to 'borrow' from their husbands, but Morris (1990) concludes that, in general, the lower the woman's earnings, the more likely they are to be necessary for the survival of the household.

The way in which money is earned, acquired, and spent, therefore, reflects both the balance of power and strains and tensions within the household, and changes in patterns of money management might reasonably be taken as an indicator of changes in the nature of gender relations within the household more generally. Pahl's original study was of 102 households, a relatively small number. She found that, where household income is low, the finances are likely to be controlled and managed by the wife. At higher incomes, particularly if the husband is the only earner, the husband is likely to control finances, with part management delegated to the wife. Where both partners earn, management is likely to be shared, although overall control still reflects relative earning power. Where a wife controls the money a household is likely to spend a higher proportion of its income on housekeeping, and money earned by wives is more likely to be spent on food and daily living expenses than is money earned by husbands. Inequality outside the household was linked to inequality in decision-making within the household, and husbands were more likely to dominate decision-making where the wife did not have a job.

A later study incorporated a greater number of households (1,211: Vogler and Pahl 1993). Although the time between the two studies was only a short one, it had been one of very rapid social change. As we saw in Chapter 2, between 1981 and 1987 there had been a very rapid loss of men's jobs and an increase in men's rates of unemployment as a consequence of recession and economic restructuring, whilst women's employment—particularly part-time employment—had carried on rising. These changes, as well as the nature and size of the two different

Table 4.4 Household money management: a comparison of different studies

	(1989*)%	(1993*)%
Female whole wage	14	26
Male whole wage	—	10
Housekeeping allowance	22	12
Pool	56	50
Independent management	9	2
Number	101	1,211

*dates of publication
Source: Vogler and Pahl (1993: 76)

Table 4.5 Household allocative systems showing different forms of pooling, and standardized household income per month

	%	£ per month
Female whole wage	27	624
Female-managed pool	15	658
Housekeeping allowance	13	697
Joint pool	20	719
Male-managed pool	15	728
Male whole wage	10	755

Source: adapted from Vogler and Pahl (1993: 77, 79)

samples, were reflected in changes in the pattern of household management.

Table 4.4 shows the continuing decline of the housekeeping allowance system as more wives go into employment, and an increase in the proportion of whole-wage systems. The proportion of households classifying themselves as pooling resources was similar. This second study found, however, that in many of the households where joint or pooling systems were claimed, in fact one or other of the couple, but not both, managed the resources, although both had access to all of the household's funds. Vogler and Pahl therefore divided the pooling systems into three types: pools managed largely by husbands, pools managed largely by wives, and those managed by both partners. This produced a six-fold classification of household allocative systems, as shown in Table 4.5.

It can be seen that female-managed systems and housekeeping allowances were associated with lower income groups. In these systems wives had experienced more intensive recent cuts in their living standards, and had less personal spending money, than their husbands (it will be remembered that this study had been carried out against a background of quite severe economic recession). This study confirmed, therefore, the association between low household incomes and a prevalence of female budgeting that had been noted in previous studies. The joint-pool system was the most egalitarian in terms of both living standards and access to personal spending money, and male-managed systems were not associated with lower living standards for men.

The most significant finding was that households in which wives were in full-time employment were much more likely to be associated with egalitarian management systems—that is, pooling—than were other households. In households where both partners were in full-time employment, 62 per cent had a pooling system, whereas only 45 per cent of households with a full-time husband and non-working wife, and only 48 per cent of households in which the husband worked and the wife had a part-time job, had pooling systems. Part-time work for the woman, therefore, would seem to have little impact on the allocation of money within the household. Vogler and Pahl's findings, therefore, confirm Morris's conclusion that 'financial equality depends on a wife's full-time employment, since part-time work simply operates to reduce calls on the husband's wage, without ever increasing wives' influence over finances' (1990: 80).

In summary, therefore, these studies support a relatively strong version of the resource theory of power in households. The more a woman contributes to the household income, the more likely she is to have an equal say in the allocation of the household's resources. Women's employment as such (that is, part-time work) does not have a particularly large impact. Thus, although change is taking place in both the domestic division of labour, and in the distribution of power and management of resources within the household, it is happening relatively slowly.

Summary and Conclusions

This chapter has explored some of the changes in both family structure and family life which have developed in parallel with the increase in women's paid employment. We have seen that many women are delaying having children, and that divorce rates and single parenthood are both rising. We have seen that the major growth in the employment of women has been amongst the mothers of young children, and that these mothers are more likely to be in relationships, and to be relatively well-educated. Childcare arrangements, except for very young children, are overwhelmingly informal, but the fact that more mothers of under-fives are working has meant an increase in the level of paid (or 'professional') childcare. This has meant an increase in (mainly) low-level jobs.

We have also touched upon the changing nature of the relationship between the sexes. Some sociologists (Giddens 1992; Beck and Beck-Gernsheim 1995) have argued that important changes in the nature of the relationships between men and women are taking place. Giddens writes of 'the democratising of personal life' (1992: 188), in which individuals can realize their own autonomy and independence whilst respecting the rights of others. Beck and Beck-Gernsheim have argued for the need to find 'new ways' of living family life in order to adapt to the changes in the gender division of labour. These would include lessening some paid-work pressures by shortening the working week, and (like Giddens) changing family relationships to make them more egalitarian.

However, in Britain it would seem that changes in the pattern of paid employment have led to growing social polarization rather than 'new ways of living'. Some households have 'too much' work—especially if both parents are in full-time employment and there are young children; some households have no paid work at all. Some people might argue that this means that we should return to the old nuclear-family model of the male breadwinner and the non-working wife. There are many reasons why this would be neither possible nor a good idea, but here we will focus on only two:

- growing inequalities in paid work overall have been the result of the deliberate deregulation and marketization of British society, rather than the expansion of women's employment as such.
- the weight of evidence points to the fact that egalitarian gender relationships within the family are very closely associated with more equal statuses *outside* the family, in particular whether or not the woman is in paid employment. Full-time employment for women is associated with both a greater sharing of domestic work, as well as more equal relationships on the important matter of household budgeting.

Changes within the household, therefore, are taking place, even if only slowly. The woman's employment status, in particular, whether she works full-time or not, seems to be very important here. Husbands of full-time working wives take a greater share of the domestic work, and full-time working wives are more likely to have or share control of money and decision-making within the household.[3] These kinds of findings lend support to the resource theory of power in the household—that is, the more resources a woman brings into the household, the more likely she is to experience an equal relationship within it.

It is also the case that the findings reviewed in this chapter lend broad support to a *materialist* understanding of the position of women and the relationship between the sexes, as discussed in Chapter 1.[4] That is, it would seem that although the economic 'balance' between the sexes does not absolutely determine the nature of relationships within the household, it has a very important impact indeed. In Chapter 5, therefore, we will examine more closely the nature of women's experiences in the world of paid work itself.

Chapter Five

Women as Employees

Introduction

We began this book with an outline of the different theories which have been developed to explain the structuring of women's work and its division between the domestic sphere and paid employment. We reviewed the arguments of Hartmann (1982) and Walby (1986), who have suggested that the main reason for women's subordinate position in the labour force is to be found in the workings of the system of patriarchy—that is, men's domination of women. These writers argue that men as individuals, and masculine institutions, operate to keep women in poorly paid positions in the workplace so that they may carry out domestic labour for their male providers. We saw that the historical bases of Hartmann and Walby's arguments have been challenged by other feminists, such as Humphries (1984), who have interpreted the nineteenth-century restrictions on women's (and children's) labour as part of a struggle by the working class to raise the returns to paid work in general by restricting its supply. It was emphasized, however, that these kinds of debate were taking place within a framework in which both 'sides' were using broadly materialist or structuralist explanations, in which human behaviour is seen as shaped to a considerable extent by institutional and contextual factors.

In Chapter 1, these kinds of explanation were contrasted with individualistic explanations which give priority to individual choice over structural constraint. For example, economists have explained the 'male-breadwinner' model by arguing that, at the level of the household, women choose to specialize in domestic work and men choose to specialize in market work. This choice is rational because men have greater investments in 'human capital' and earn more than women. These arguments are problematic. Can women be said to 'choose' domestic work if their opportunities outside the household are worse than those of men? Nevertheless, they have been recently restated by Hakim (1996), who also emphasizes the overriding significance of choice. She argues that the pattern of women's employment reflects the fact that there are two different types of women, the committed and the uncommitted, and it is the uncommitted women who are in part-time and low-level jobs. In Chapter 1 we also looked at recent feminist theories which, although taking a very different theoretical perspective from that of Hakim, share with her an emphasis upon the extent of difference and variation within the category of 'woman'.

In the following chapters we carried over this focus on the broad structuring of women's employment into a description of the situation in the 1990s. We examined patterns of occupational segregation by sex, and of characteristically 'female' employment patterns such as part-time work and homework. We found that, whilst it was indeed the case that many such women are 'satisfied' with their employment, one major reason for their taking it was to be able to combine paid work with domestic work, which is still seen by many (men and women) as women's main priority. However, the organization of domestic and caring work is not the same in all countries, and in Chapter 3 we saw how variations in national institutions (particularly the welfare state, and the state's policies in relation to women and children) have had an important impact on the structuring of women's paid employment at the aggregate level. These cross-national differences would suggest that structural factors are very important.

In Chapter 4 we continued with our examination of the employment–household interface, focusing on Britain in particular. We found that, with the increase in the amount of women's market work, there had been some increase in the amount of men's domestic work—although the process of change is clearly very slow. However, we also found that changes in the domestic division of labour, and in women's relative power within the household, were greatest when women were in full-time work.

In the first part of the book, our discussions operated largely at the macro level of analysis, examining aggregate-level employment patterns and cross-national differences. In Chapter 4, however, we have also examined the micro level of the household. In this chapter we will continue with this more detailed focus and examine the employment experience of women in more depth. We will also be exploring more systematically research on women's employment which has been influenced by recent debates in feminist theory.

Women's Paid Work

Three different, but interwoven, themes may be identified in commentaries on the study of women's employment since the 1970s:

- There was already an established tradition in the sociology of work and industrial sociology which had worked on the assumption that 'workers' were 'men'. For example, one of the most influential British studies of the 1960s, *The Affluent Worker: Industrial Attitudes and Behaviour* (Goldthorpe *et al.* 1968) had only interviewed men. With the increase in women's employment and the growing influence of second-wave feminism, this strategy came under increasing criticism. One major theme of 'second-wave' feminism in the 1970s, therefore, was that of identifying the 'invisible' woman within the sociology of work, as well as making explicit the existing taken-for-granted assumptions in the study of women and work.
- Because social scientists had implicitly assumed that women's domestic roles and responsibilities were largely 'natural', women's inferior labour-market position had been seen to be largely a result of these domestic responsibilities. However, the identification of the 'invisible woman' within the workplace resulted in an increasing emphasis upon the significance of *employment*-related and -located factors in explaining women's subordinate position within the workplace. This second theme, therefore, has focused upon how the structuring of organizational and labour processes (Braverman 1974) has shaped women's, and men's, employment.
- Recent studies of the workplace from a gender perspective, however, have moved away from an emphasis on the *structural* determining of jobs and employment towards an emphasis upon the *meanings and discourses*—including gender discourses—which constitute workplaces, and the roles (jobs) of people within them. This work draws upon the recent developments in feminist theory discussed in Chapter 1, in particular the debates around 'difference' (Barrett 1987).

In the next sections of this chapter we will use these three themes to organize our discussion of the contemporary situation of women as employees.

The 'Invisible Woman'

Industrial sociology and the sociology of work in the 1950s and 1960s had laid very heavy emphasis upon studies of male employees and male-only workplaces. In part this was a reflection of the nature of the perceived 'problems' which were being investigated in these studies—levels of industrial strife and conflict and its manifestations, such as strike rates; output restrictions (that is, failing to work hard or produce enough); negative attitudes to work; problems in adjusting to technical change, and so on. Thus predominantly masculine, usually manual workplaces and occupational groups were extensively studied—miners, dockworkers, car workers, printers, and shipbuilders. Women were in a small minority in these industries. In any case, on account of their 'natural' docility, women workers were not seen as being as likely to engage in industrial conflict, or present a problem for management, to the same extent as men.

When women as employees were investigated there was a tendency to treat them as 'unisex' (Brown 1976). Findings from studies of men (or women) were generalized to apply to all employees. Officially 'the worker' had no gender, but in fact that gender was masculine. This assumption that workers were 'unisex' can be seen very clearly in a classic study of industrial sociology of the 1930s, the Hawthorne Experiments (Roethlisberger and Dickson 1947). This study examined two different work groups, the Bank Wiring Room and the Relay Assembly Test Room, located in the same factory in the Hawthorne plant of the Bell Telephone Company (US). In the Bank Wiring Room, despite the fact that the workers got more pay the more that they produced, the work group co-operated so as to restrict their level of output and thus protect their jobs. They reasoned that if they increased their levels of production the managers would use this as an excuse to reduce the numbers of the workforce. However, in the Relay Assembly Test Room (RATR) the workers responded to a series of experimental changes in their working arrangements (such as in the timing of rest periods, lengthening and shortening the working day, adding and removing incentives) by constantly increasing their output, rather than restricting it. The researchers argued that this apparently inexplicable finding (of constantly rising productivity despite variations in experimental conditions) was because the RATR workers had been made to 'feel special' by being the subject of an experiment and had responded positively. They also argued that the 'friendly supervision' in the Test Room had also had an important impact.

What was not emphasized by the Hawthorne researchers, however, was that all of the workers in the Bank Wiring Room were men, whereas all of the workers in the RATR were women.[1] Moreover, they were young, unmarried women from traditional patriarchal (immigrant family) backgrounds, and all of their supervisors, as well as the researchers who were observing them, were men. Acker and Van Houten (1974) have argued that their youth and social backgrounds made these young women very responsive to the paternalistic treatment they received during the experiment:

the relationship was between powerful males and weak females; that is, the females, being weak, had to please the supervisors if they wished to stay in the test room (two 'troublemakers' were removed and replaced during the course of the experiment), so they adopted the norm of increased production . . . compliance led to special rewards. (1974: 156)

Thus is may be argued that the 'Hawthorne effect' (the positive consequences of friendly supervision and being made to 'feel special') is in reality a 'gender effect'. However, it has been described and applied in gender-neutral terms, and the 'Hawthorne effect' went on to inform practice for several generations of personnel managers.

In other circumstances and studies women employees *were* seen as being a 'problem', although the problems they presented were not the same as those of men. Women's problems stemmed from their 'two roles', at home and work (Yudkin and Holme 1963). Whereas the idea of *men* in paid work presented no difficulties in the 1950s and 1960s, there was seen to be something problematic about women, especially married women, in paid employment. These kinds of assumption, of course, reflected the dominance of the 'male-breadwinner' model in the social sciences, as well as in assumptions about social life more generally.

In many studies, therefore, sex-segregated models were in operation in the sociological analysis of work as employment right into the 1970s and 1980s. Feldberg and Glenn (1979) have described these as the 'job model', which was applied to studies of men, and the 'gender model', which was used in studies of women. In the 'job model', the work people do—their employment—is seen as the primary factor explaining their behaviour both on and off the job. Thus miners, for example, are characterized by relatively high levels of industrial conflict on the job and tight-knit social networks off the job. This is a consequence of the unpleasant and dangerous nature of their work (Dennis *et al.* 1969; Gouldner 1954). In contrast, the 'gender model' ignores the kind of work that women do and explains their relationship to employment in terms of their personal characteristics, their family situation, and so on. The two models have been summarized in Table 5.1.

As Feldberg and Glenn argued, this implicit job/gender, male/female model had both distorted the interpretation of existing research findings—for example, women's behaviour at work was seen as being a

Table 5.1 The sociology of work in the 1970s

Assumptions	Job Model	Gender Model
Basic social relationships determined by:	Work (employment)	Family
Family structure:	Male-headed, nuclear	Male-headed, nuclear
Connection to family is:	As economic provider/worker	As wife/mother
Social position determined by:	Work	Family
Sociopolitical behaviour and attitudes derived from:	Occupational socialization, class/status of occupation, social relations of work	Gender role socialization, family roles, activities, and relationships of household work
Central life interest is in:	Employment and earnings	Family

Source: Feldberg and Glenn (1979: 527)

consequence of their domestic roles, rather than of the negative aspects of the jobs they did—but also as biasing the direction of research: 'The job-gender paradigm defines job conditions as problematic for men and family responsibilities as problematic for women, thereby directing research into these areas' (p. 532).

Feldberg and Glenn called for a new approach to the study of women and work. Such an approach, they suggested, should include domestic work and unpaid caring as 'work', as well as bringing the investigation of the processes of gender stratification into the analysis of work itself. In fact, as we have already seen in this book and as we shall discuss further in the next section of this chapter, subsequent research on women's employment has been much concerned with these issues.

Women's Work, Organizations, and Labour Processes

In the 1950s the US sociologist Caplow (1954) argued that women's employment was organized around two central cultural themes:

- That it is disgraceful for a man to be directly subordinated to a woman, except in family or sexual relationships.

- That intimate groups, except those based on family or sexual ties, should be composed of either sex but never both.

The first theme relates to hierarchical relations within the organization of paid work, the second to the clustering of men and women into different jobs. After second-wave feminism and equality legislation these two assertions might look distinctly old-fashioned. Nevertheless, both have been very important in structuring women's employment. Cultural themes, however, do not simply hang in mid-air, but more usually reflect imbalances of power and authority. This first theme reflects the historical domination of men over women. It is manifested in the fact that women predominate in lower-level jobs, and men in higher-level jobs, that is, vertical occupational segregation. The second theme reflects the fact that some jobs come to be seen as 'women's' jobs, and some to be seen as 'men's' (horizontal segregation). Indeed, as we have seen in Chapter 2, within the workplace men have a greater tendency to work with men, and women with women. This might be described as the 'cultural gendering' of occupations, and is a feature of many traditional industries which are themselves in decline. For example, in the cotton industry, one of the foremost industries which developed in Britain in the Industrial Revolution, women did the work of preparation (carding and cleaning), whilst men were responsible for spinning.

However, once it is recognized that the domination of women by men incorporates relations of power rather than being simply 'natural' or 'cultural', we can see that these themes are closely related. Men have excluded women from particular jobs, and it has simultaneously been claimed that the job is 'unsuitable' for a woman. Once a task has been defined as a 'female' occupation, then it is very often defined as unskilled, or lacking in importance, as compared to 'male' jobs. During the 1970s and 1980s, studies of the labour process in different occupations and industries illustrated these processes. For example, Game and Pringle (1984) described how, in 'white goods' manufacturing (washing machines, refrigerators, and so on) a set of descriptive contrasts was used to define the difference between men's and women's work. Men's work was held to be skilled, heavy, dirty, and requiring mobility; women's work was held to be unskilled, light, clean, and sedentary. Technological change made men's work less skilled: skilled machinists, for example, had their jobs taken over by automated technology. Automated presses and robots had eliminated heavy and dangerous jobs. In short, men's work became more like women's work. However women were not moved into men's jobs. Rather, yet another distinction, that between the technical and non-technical, was introduced in order to justify the ongoing sexual division of labour.

Cultural gendering, therefore, is often bound up with direct and indirect masculine exclusionary practices. The nature of the employers' demand for labour is also important in shaping the gender composition of the workforce within organizations. For example, both Coyle (1982) in the case of the clothing industry, and Glucksmann (1990) in the case of light assembly work, have shown how the employers' pursuit of cheap labour has created low level 'women's' jobs.

The effects of both the nature of employer *demand* and the operation of masculine exclusionary practices can be identified in the case of the banking industry (Crompton and Jones 1984; Crompton 1989; Crompton and Sanderson 1990). The financial sector, of which banking is a major part, has been a major source of employment growth for both men and women over the last fifty years.[2] It provides a particularly apt example of the way in which gendered processes within the organization have interacted with external developments in gender relations and the position of women, that is, in the nature of the female labour *supply*. The industry will be used as a recurring point of reference throughout this chapter. Right up into the 1980s, the banks were the classic locus of the 'bureaucratic' career. The clearing banks (old-established banks such as Lloyds, the Midland, Natwest, and Barclays[3]) relied for their labour force on the recruitment of well-qualified school leavers, who were then trained by the bank and promoted through the ranks to managerial positions.[4] The banks operated an informal 'no poaching' policy in respect of each other's career staff, so that a move to another bank was not an option for a disappointed careerist. The network of retail branches provided the physical framework for the bureaucratic career, and young clerks on their way up would often move from branch to branch as they progressed.

Bureaucratic careers in banking, however, were in practice available only to young men, even though the numbers of young women recruited by the clearing banks had been rising steadily. Technological change (in particular, the introduction of computers and the expansion of Information Technology) meant that arithmetic and accountancy skills were becoming less and less important, and much routine clerical work was computerized throughout the 1970s. The demand for low-level clerical labour expanded rapidly from the 1960s. The banks responded to this situation by recruiting large numbers of young women, the vast majority of whom left at the birth of their first child. This short-term, feminized, low-level clerical labour force, therefore, left bureaucratic careers through the different grade levels in banking still open to men—a pattern which was repeated in other industries, such as insurance and local government (Crompton and Jones 1984).

Here we have a good example, therefore, of employer demand helping to generate and perpetuate a mass, feminized, clerical labour force. However, the banks' demand for a particular type of clerical labour also ran in parallel with masculine exclusionary practices. Until the 1960s sex discrimination in banking was quite explicit. Up until the 1950s young women had to formally resign from the bank on getting married (they would usually be immediately reappointed on a non-career grade), and separate salary scales for men and women persisted into the 1960s. Explicit discriminatory rules had been removed by the end of the 1960s; but nevertheless a number of other practices served to keep women out of managerial grades. Young female recruits were openly discouraged from taking the professional examinations (of the Institute of Bankers) necessary for promotion. All banks had a geographical mobility agreement—that is, those wishing to be promoted had to agree to be geographically mobile—which indirectly discriminated against women. More particularly, individual managers (all men) made it very obvious, in their handling of staff, that it was the young men who would get promotion, not the women (Crompton and Jones 1984).

As a result of these direct and indirect discriminatory practices, Barclays Bank was referred to the Equal Opportunities Commission in 1983. It must be stressed that Barclays was not the exception here: as a manager in another bank said shortly afterwards: 'There but for the grace of God goes all of us' (Crompton 1989). The referral issue centred directly on recruitment practices, that is, the demand for labour. As we have seen, the banks were operating an informal two-tier recruiting system, and 'of the applicants with GCE A-Levels a higher proportion of males were successful than females, and the situation was the reverse for applicants at O-Level' (Crompton 1989: 148). As a result of this referral, Barclays began to monitor their recruitment procedures in order to demonstrate that they were non-discriminatory. In practice, all of the major clearing banks began to pay especial attention to their Equal Opportunities practices. Today many banks are at the leading edge of Equal Opportunities employment. For example, the Midland Bank was amongst the first of the large companies to introduce a workplace nurseries scheme, and many of the banks have joined 'Opportunity 2000', a government-sponsored scheme to get more women into managerial positions.

It might appear, therefore, that we have here a straightforward example of legislative pressure having the desired effect, and that the banks, who were once amongst the most 'backward' of employers as far as sex equality was concerned, have now been transformed. Most banks have high-profile Equal Opportunities policies. To varying degrees, all of the major banks have introduced extended maternity leaves, leave to care for sick children (available to either parent), and opportunities for job-sharing (that is, a situation in which two people share one job and both work part-time).

There have indeed been important changes in employment practices in banks and the financial sector as far as gender is concerned. However, it would not be correct to see these as being just a consequence of pressure from the Equal Opportunities Commission. The nature of work in banking has itself been transformed over the last ten years, and with it the nature of the employer's demand for labour. There has been increased competition in the financial sector because of the fact that a range of other institutions are now able to offer banking services, and building societies, insurance companies, and even supermarkets are now able to operate as banks. Technological change has simplified, and speeded up banking services, and it is now possible to bank entirely by telephone. In consequence, branch banking has been simplified, and much routine bank work is done by lower-level clerks in regional processing centres. For an increasing number of bank workers, their jobs have shifted more and more to the activity of selling.

As a result, the old-style bank career of everyone being recruited at the same level, and being trained and promoted 'through the ranks', has gone. The informal two-tier recruiting system has been regularized, and banks now recruit at different levels in order to meet their different needs—clerical, management trainees, graduate trainees, and so on. People recruited on clerical grades can no longer expect to be groomed for management, particularly if they are recruited to one of the major processing centres. Women still predominate in the lowest clerical grades but, because they have not been recruited into positions associated with any expectation of promotion beyond a fairly low level, masculine exclusionary practices are not necessary in order to keep them out.[5]

In the case of banking, therefore, we can see that, first, the nature of employer demand, and second, a history of both indirect and explicit masculine exclusionary practices, have served to create a labour force that was typically gendered—women carrying out low-level clerical work, men in supervisory and management positions. In short, it is not too difficult to see how structural factors—the organization of the labour process and the demand for labour, rules governing promotion (such as the geographical mobility clause), and male exclusionary practices—have all made a major contribution to the unequal position of female employees within the banking sector. However, despite the reforms of recent years, women remain by far the greater majority of those in low-level positions in banking, for the simple reason that women are the majority of the applicants for the lower-level jobs. In short, it would seem that there are limits to structural explanations for the unequal employment situation of women in comparison to men in the banking industry. Perhaps because of this fact, in recent years the study of women and employment has moved beyond a consideration of the structural constraints on women in the workplace in order to examine the way in which different kinds of 'gender' are actively constructed within the workplace.[6] This shift also reflects recent developments in feminist theory.

Gender Meanings and Discourses in Employment

This kind of approach to the study of women and employment seeks not so much to identify the kinds of organizational and work-group structures which are held to 'determine' the position and behaviour of men and women within the workplace, as to understand employment and organizational contexts through demonstrating how particular kinds of masculinities and femininities, and discourses of gender, are created within the workplace. The term 'discourse' is being used here in a relatively straightforward fashion to mean a series of linked meanings which together create a 'subject'. For example, Pringle (1988) argues that:

The question of 'what is a secretary' may be answered with reference to three discourses which have coexisted, at times peacefully and at others in open competition with each other. The first of these, the 'office wife' is strongly middle-class and may be found in 'serious' . . . teaching manuals. The second, the 'sexy secretary', became the dominant one in the 1950s and 60s. . . . It relates to . . . popular culture, particularly the tabloids . . . its central theme is the mindless Dolly Bird. . . . The third discourse, the 'career woman' derives from a variety of approaches. (p. 5)

In other words, the answer to the question 'what is a secretary' can have different meanings depending upon the discourse being used, and each 'discourse' has its particular sets of meanings and/or stereotypes. The way in which we describe something, or talk about it, signifies the way it is: for 'post-structuralists', language is central. Rather than focusing upon the individual as such, and how he or she 'reacts' to structural constraint(s), the emphasis has shifted to the way in which different kinds of men and women are 'produced' within an organizational context.

This kind of approach to the study of gender and employment draws upon the recent developments in feminist theory which were briefly sketched in Chapter 1. Ideas about the development of masculinities and femininities have taken insights from psychoanalytic accounts of how people become 'male' and 'female'. For example, Nancy Chodorow (1978, 1989) has argued that one of the reasons why men develop 'masculine' characteristics such as emotional control and distancing is because, in order to become men, they have to achieve a separation from their first carer, the mother. Thus 'men' have to become 'not feminine'. The recent emphasis upon different discourses of 'work' also draws upon a particular strand of 'difference' feminism which has stressed the extent of difference *within* the category of 'woman'.

Recent feminist theory can also be loosely identified with the theoretical approach known as 'post-modernism', an approach which has de-emphasized the idea of 'structure' and 'big explanations' (or 'metanarratives'), and has emphasized instead the uncertain, culturally depthless, endlessly reconstructed nature of the contemporary world. For example, post-modern organization theory focuses upon how organization is produced and reproduced, rather than on how organizational structures can be identified, understood, and improved (Hearn *et al.* 1989: 17). Organizations are viewed as a 'process' rather than as a 'structure'. The classic model of bureaucracy developed by Max Weber stressed, above all, the rational and impersonal nature of bureaucratic *structures,* within which asexual, undifferentiated bodies or individuals are located or fitted. In contrast, 'post-modern' approaches to organizational analysis emphasize the social *structuring* of the body/bodies within the organizational context.

These developments in discussions and analyses of gender and employment reflect recent developments in approaches to social theory more generally. The issues raised are complex, and it is not possible to investigate them adequately here. Nevertheless, although we will not enter fully into the debates in social and feminist theory they raise, the position being taken in this book should be made explicit.

First, it should be acknowledged that these 'post-structuralist' approaches have resulted in a number of important insights in respect of particular aspects of gender and employment. For example, the stress on viewing organizations as not only or simply rational structures means that we can better understand not only how bureaucracy generates particular kinds of masculinities and femininities, but also how sexuality—through sexual harassment, for example—can be used as an instrument of control. Recognizing the diversity of discourses that go to make up our images of male and female employees enlarges our understandings of actual situations, and should make us careful of over-generalizing about 'all men' or 'all women'. However, we also have to be careful to remember that although our understandings may have been enhanced by recognizing the importance of discourse in shaping our view of reality, nevertheless there is also a world of institutional structure and constraints, and these have real effects. For example, as Maynard (1995) has argued:

> our lived experience is mediated not just through discourse or text but through material structures and relationships also. These may range from family and friends, to access to knowledge and learning, to the amount of money, food and other resources which are available. Such things need to be taken into account because of the ways in which they influence how men and women may be restricted or empowered in their everyday lives. It is, therefore, necessary to assert that (notwithstanding the significance of culture and discourse) events, relations and social formations do have conditions of existence and real effects outside the sphere of the discursive and that these need to be investigated. (pp. 275–6)

In the rest of this section, therefore, we will examine in brief two recent examples of the 'post-structuralist' study of women's employment: Pringle's (1988) work on secretaries, and Halford *et al.*'s (1995) research on banking. We will then discuss the topic of sexual harassment. Finally, we will return to a broader consideration of the interaction of structures and cultures, discourse and constraint, in a consideration of the recent entry of women into higher-level professions and occupations.

In the previous section of this chapter we have seen how the employment situation of women in the British clearing banks has been shaped by the employer's need for a particular kind of labour (low-level clerical work), and maintained by a series of organizational rules and practices which kept women out of higher-level positions. We have also noted how both increased competition and technical change have radically altered the nature of employment in banking for both men and women, giving much more emphasis to a culture of competition and selling. Halford *et al.* (1995) develop the notion of 'embodied restructuring' in order to give an account of this process, suggesting that organizational restructuring and gendering processes cannot, in practice, be separated from each other. These authors are attempting to move away from a position which focuses mainly on the demand for labour (a 'structural' factor), to one which emphasizes the extent to which organizational restructuring is centrally concerned with changing *people*.

Much of this 'embodied restructuring' centred on the role of the male manager (in this discussion we will, for a change, focus upon masculinity rather than femininity!). The traditional male bank manager was a sober, reliable, paternalistic figure, well-known in the local community (a comic stereotype of this role is to be found in the figure of Captain Mainwaring in the television programme 'Dad's Army'). This kind of safe, respectable behaviour—in personal life as well as in employment [7]—was reinforced by the bureaucratic career structure in which years of good behaviour would be rewarded by eventual promotion (Crompton and Jones 1984). Promotion was administered 'from the top', the progress of individuals was monitored, and at a suitable moment they would be 'appointed' to a higher grade. The sober and respectable image of the bank manager was reinforced by the physical surroundings of branch banking, which once consisted of wood-panelled offices, mahogany counters, and separate offices for senior staff.

In the new sales culture (Halford and Savage give their case study the pseudonym of 'Sellbank'), not only have banks been transformed into bright and attractive sales areas, but also a new kind of manager has had to be created:

Managers are now set annual targets, given performance related pay and are expected to apply for jobs rather than be promoted to them unasked . . . the new managerial virtues (are) being . . . forward looking and 'change masters' . . . the new managerial culture endorses the attributes of 'competitive masculinity' which . . . sustains a hierarchy imbued with instrumentalism, careerism . . . productivism and risk taking. (1995: 109)

Halford and Savage suggest that it is no accident that 'those areas of management (in Sellbank) where the virtues of "performance", hard work and competitiveness are most celebrated are those which have the highest proportion of male managers' (p. 110). Competitiveness, therefore, has replaced stability and paternalism as the quality of the ideal bank manager—and these superior qualities are closely associated with male-dominated areas of banking such as corporate lending.

Our discussion has focused on women's employment in banking because it is an industry in which the wider social changes over the last few decades—in the world of employment, and in gender relations—can be seen in operation. We have seen how the industry both reflected and reproduced particular patterns of gender relations over the years, from the traditional male-breadwinner model of the 1940s and 1950s, in which an all-male management acted as paterfamilias over a largely masculine labour force of young clerks and other subordinate men, to the 1960s and 1970s, in which the mass clerical labour force became dominated by a short-term, feminized labour force. These changes, however, still left the traditional bureaucratic career largely intact. In the last phase, increased competition and the selling culture has begun to erode the stability of the bureaucratic career itself. All three phases were reflected in varying sets of assumptions about aspects of the domestic sphere. In the first phase, a man was expected to be married, but not to be married too young; responsible, respectable domestic behaviour was expected. In the second phase, the relatively well-educated young women who formed the mass clerical labour force were expected to leave the bank when their first child was born—and the vast majority did. In the third phase, it is anticipated that although some individual women will want careers and promotion (reflecting the erosion of the 'male-breadwinner' model), it is assumed that most will wish to earn a 'component wage'—that is, a wage which makes a substantial contribution to, but does not fully support, a household (Siltanen 1986). The banks are now in the forefront of 'family-friendly' policies which allow women to do this.

Paid employment and domestic life, therefore, can be seen to have been meshed together in different ways over both the passage of historical time and the requirements of the domestic life-cycle. However, these interconnections are made not just at the level of practicalities. Sexual and familial-related discourses are also involved in the construction of relationships of power and authority within the workplace itself. This observation, of course, is not peculiar to discourse analysis as such, as we have seen in our discussion of reinterpretations of the Hawthorne experiments. Studies of early industrialization in Britain showed how young female workers were subject to quite explicit patriarchal controls (Lown 1983), and in a parallel fashion, Elson (1991) and others have pointed to the fact that in the 'tiger economies' of the Pacific Rim, many factories draw almost entirely on the labour of young women. Such workers have 'nimble fingers' and are held to be particularly suitable for precision assembly work in the electronics industry. Their subordination within traditional families and 'natural' submissiveness makes them even more suitable for this kind of work, which requires high levels of concentration and close attention to detail.

Pringle's work on secretaries goes beyond these general observations to demonstrate how the home/work discourse organizes interpersonal authority relations in the workplace. As we have noted above, classic studies of bureaucracy have emphasized the rationality and impersonality of bureaucratic organization. Against this background, an early and influential study of gender and organizations, Kanter's *Men and Women of the Corporation* (1977), suggested that the boss–secretary relationship, because of what is often its intensely personal nature, was a 'patrimonial relic' within a rational bureaucratic shell (secretaries often moved jobs with bosses, carried out personal services for them, and so on). She suggested that, as an out-of-date bureaucratic anomaly, this kind of work relationship would eventually be eroded as women gained more power within organizations and rejected this kind of subordination. However, rather than seeing them as an anomaly, Pringle argues that sexual and family relationships are central to the understanding of power relations within the workplace. In her study of secretarial work, she found among the boss–secretary relationships she investigated a number of different discourses between men and women, and women and women. These included father/daughter; mother/son; mother/daughter; and wife-cum-mistress. She argues:

Relationships run most smoothly where each accepts the 'natural' authority of the man over the woman. This is seen as so natural that a power relation is barely percieved to exist—which minimises overt conflict. This is not to say that women are powerless. But when they do claim authority it is in family terms, as mothers, for example, rather than as women. Their authority has a limited domain. (1988: 216)

We have returned full circle, therefore, to Caplow's (1954) 'central cultural theme': 'that it is disgraceful for a man to be subordinated to a woman, except in family or sexual relationships'. Discourse analysis demonstrates the manner in which power and sexuality operate through interpersonal relations between men and women to create particular kinds of masculinities and femininities. In the next section of this chapter, we will examine a particularly overt manifestation of this power—sexual harassment.

Sexual Harassment

This is a highly contentious area, not least because sexuality and associated behaviours are often highly enjoyable, and the line between 'recreational' and 'harassing' sexual behaviour may be seen to be blurred and unstable. High-profile stories, usually concerning the experiences of women in traditionally masculine occupational environments, such as the police or the armed forces, constantly hit the headlines. At the time of writing, the case of a young ex-servicewoman who has just lost her case at an industrial tribunal has been the subject of much comment—she claimed that her promotion prospects had been affected by harrassing behaviour aboard ship. At sea women are to be found in a very small minority, and are likely to be intimidated in a masculine culture in which porn movies, heavy drinking, and sexist jokes are commonplace (Chandler *et al.* 1995). What may be 'normal' for many men may be experienced as harassment by many, if not most, women. Sexual harassment functions particularly to keep women out of non-traditional occupations, and to reinforce their secondary status in the workplace.

Gutek (1989) has used the term 'sex role spillover' to describe the carry-over of gender-based expectations into the workplace. Among the role characteristics that have been associated with 'femaleness' is being a sex object:

Women are expected to be sexual and to elicit sexual overtures from men rather naturally. In a 32-nation study of sex stereotypes, the characteristics of sexy, affectionate, and attractive were associated with femaleness. What is . . . important is the fact the *there is no strongly held comparable belief about men* . . . the cluster of characteristics that are usually associated with the male personality does not include a sexual component. Rather the stereotype of men revolves around the dimension of competence and activity. (pp. 59–60; emphasis in the original)

In the workplace, sex-role spillover has the effect of making a women highly visible as sexual objects. Women's percieved sexuality can be seen as being more important than their work roles, and in order to avoid being cast in the role of a sex object, women may attempt to act in a completely asexual manner. They will then run the risk of being described as 'frigid', a prude, or a lesbian. It is seen as the woman's responsibility to 'manage' sexuality within an organizational context, and women tend to be blamed if things 'get out of hand'.

In contrast, men's sexuality is not as visible. Unlike women, men are seen as 'natural' inhabitants of organizations; they are seen as goal-oriented, rational, competitive, and assertive beings. If men do behave in an overtly sexual manner, this is seen as being a characteristic of the individual in question, rather than of all men. Indeed, sexual pursuit by individual men may even be seen positively, as an element of masculine goal-oriented behaviour. Studies comparing different workplaces have shown that harassment is more likely when women are in 'non-traditional', that is, men's occupations (DiTomaso 1989). We can draw upon a recent study of sexual harassement in a non-traditional occupation—insurance sales—in order to illustrate the points that have been made so far.

In the life-assurance industry, sales managers have traditionally been men. Collinson and Collinson's (1996) study reports on a company in which the only women managers in this all-male area had recently been 'lost', despite the fact that the women concerned had been highly qualified, with degrees and professional qualifications, and had (in terms of sales figures) been successful at their jobs. The authors argue that sexual harassment had been a key factor in these women losing (or leaving) their jobs.

Insurance sales depends heavily on male homosociability. Christmas lunches, conference dinners, and client entertaining are not only an integral part of the job but also a means of rewarding star performers. Male homosociability on these occasions is often intensely sexual, including competitions to see who can tell the 'dirtiest' joke, and/or to use sexist and racist jokes as 'icebreakers'. This kind of behaviour was not discouraged in the company studied. One senior manager in particular ('Dick Sharples') was well-known for his overtly sexual behaviour towards women, and had a company-wide reputation as a 'ladies' man' and a heavy drinker. Two women managers with whom he came into contact dealt with the problem in rather different ways. The first female manager recruited (Jenny) complained about Dick's behaviour, which included his regularly propositioning her for sex and leaving his flies undone. The response to her complaints was that 'it was only Dick', who everbody knew was 'like that'. Although a very high performer in terms of sales figures, Jenny's strategy of *resistance* was seen by her superiors as 'whingeing' and not being able to cope with the problem. Another female manager, Shiela, attempted to deal with the problem by *integrating* herself into the masculine culture. This meant becoming an 'honorary man', and giving as good as she got. For example, she described a situation in which Dick had gone beyond the open-flies routine and had taken out his penis to show her, suggesting that 'if she was lucky she would get some of it', Shiela felt she retained control of the situation by laughing with the other (male) representatives present and replying that 'it does not look worth having' (1996: 36).

The senior manager concerned thought that Jenny had a problem in 'handling men' and in adapting to the male-dominated sales culture. However, he thought that Shiela's personality was 'far too aggressive, too competitive, and difficult to work with'. 'He claimed that because she tried *too* hard to integrate into the male culture, she did not have the respect of the men in sales' (1996: 43). Neither resistance nor integration, therefore, had protected these women from sexual harassment; and, despite good performance figures, both were eventually made redundant.

This rather depressing story illustrates all of Gutek's arguments about sex-role spillover. Harassing behaviour by particular men is seen as a personal attribute ('it's only Dick'). The highly derogatory and sexualized atmosphere of insurance sales is seen as being a part of normal goal-oriented behaviour, and being able to take part in and handle this culture is seen as a rite of passage which women have to learn to manage. If their attempts to manage the situation are not successful—which they were not—then women must take the blame. As we have seen, both of the women discussed above were made redundant because of their failure to integrate into the particular masculine culture of insurance sales. Finally, the case study also confirms that harassment is likely in non-traditional occupations for women. An important feature of such non-traditional occupations is that they are usually associated with higher levels of power and material reward than traditional female occupations.

In short, sexual harassment continues to play an important part in keeping women in subordinate positions, although these practices are increasingly being resisted. Nevertheless, an increasing number of women are entering higher-level occupations. Does this mean that vertical occupational segregation is finally being eroded?

Women in Management and the Professions

Chapter 2 gave details of the increasing number of women entering into higher-level managerial and professional occupations over the last twenty-five years. The level of educational qualifications amongst women has been rising, and women are now more than half of all university students, and comprise half the students in other prestigious training establishments such as medical schools. Men were 80 per cent of all employers and managers in 1981, and 90 per cent of professionals. By 1991 these percentages had fallen to 71.4 per cent of employers and managers, and 81.7 per cent of (employed) professionals. As we saw in Chapter 4, this increase in the proportion of well-qualified women has also been associated with a rise in the number of such women remaining in (or returning to) paid employment when their children are young.

Women in higher-level occupations are more likely to be in those classed as 'professional' rather than 'managerial'. In particular, women are concentrated in caring and educational professions such as teaching, nursing, and social work. Savage (1992) has used census data to examine patterns of male and female mobility (that is, changes from higher-level to lower-level occupations, and vice versa) between 1971 and 1981. He showed that managers were more likely to be downwardly mobile than professionals, but that female managers were more likely to move downwards than male managers. On the basis of this evidence, he argues that 'women who enter the middle classes tend to do so in professional positions in which they can practice their expertise, but they have very limited chances of climbing a bureaucratic hierarchy through movement into managerial work' (1992: 137). In short, as the education and skill levels of women increase, so these are increasingly integrated into the labour force as women get professional jobs. Nevertheless, women still find it difficult to reach the highest levels of power in organizations. In this section, therefore, we will will focus on two occupations, one managerial (banking) and one professional (medicine).

Women have been increasing their representation at the managerial level quite rapidly over the last decade. Figures from a major clearing bank shows that whereas women were only 8 per cent of those on managerial grades in 1986, this percentage had risen to 24 per cent by 1996 (women were 55 per cent of the full-time workforce). However, the distribution of women throughout the managerial grades was far from even, and women were clustered in particular positions within management. In his study of banking, Savage (1992) also found that women managers were concentrated into particular jobs within banking. He showed that women tended to be employed as managers in units such as Head Office, and other specialist service areas, where there are a high proportion of managers overall. This finding would confirm his argument that managerial women tend to be concentrated in departments where they are mainly employed to use their skills, rather than being in positions of organizational power.

Recent figures from banking[8] show that women are also over-represented in managerial grades in retail service or processing centres, where 'management' will usually mean the supervision of other women engaged in data processing for the branch network. Women were 36 per cent of such managers. Women managers were also over-represented in telephone banking (44 per cent). Both these are areas in which there is a mass female clerical labour force which is relatively specialized but also routine. These clerical jobs are not linked to what remains of the conventional career ladder in banking in the branch network, and are located in large offices separate from the retail branch structure. The proportion of managers in these operations was not particularly high, but many of them were women engaged largely in the supervision of other women in low-level jobs.

Women managers were also over-represented in personal financial services (that is, providing financial services directly to customers), and in Head Office (31 per cent), where most provided specialist services such as, for example, personnel and Human Resource Management. The would confirm Savage's findings relating to the use of women as providers of skills, rather than as wielders of organizational power. However, women were under-represented amongst higher-level management, and the proportion of women on managerial grades declined from 33 per cent to 4 per cent from the lowest to the highest managerial grades. Women were also under-represented amongst branch managers, at only 11 per cent.

In the case of banking, therefore, we can see that although the proportions of women managers has increased within the industry, women have not simply moved into what were once 'male' jobs. Rather, as the nature of work in the industry has itself been radically transformed, so women have tended to move into female 'niches' within management. These tend to involve the provision of specialist services (that is, they are 'skill and expertise' jobs rather than 'control' jobs), or the supervision of other women (Crompton and Sanderson 1994). In general, therefore, women do not hold the positions with the highest power.

It might be thought that the situation in medicine might be different. After all, all doctors have to undergo the same kind of training, which takes many years. All doctors, men and women, therefore, are equally well-qualified. Women were kept out of medical schools until the early years of this century. Even after this restriction was lifted, female quotas, which artificially held down the number of women students, were operated by medical schools until the end of the 1960s (and beyond). These restrictions have largely been removed and women are now over 50 per cent of medical students in Britain, and 29 per cent of all doctors. However, in medicine, the increase in the number of women doctors has not been evenly spread across the medical profession.

Doctors in Britain work in two main areas: General Practice (GPs), and hospitals. About 30 per cent of all doctors are GPs. Many of the doctors working in hospitals are undergoing the last years of their training, and will eventually move into General Practice. Other doctors in hospitals are in the process of training to become specialists in particular branches of medicine—surgeons, psychiatrists, paediatricians (that is, child specialists), anaesthetists, and so on. The training to become a specialist takes many years, and many doctors do not reach the level of Consultant (top specialist) until their late thirties. Some do not reach consultant level at all, and some of these doctors will 'drop out' and become GPs. There is also a hierarchy of prestige amongst the different medical specialities. Surgery has a very high status, particularly in the more dramatic areas, such as brain surgery or organ transplants. Specialists working in other areas have less prestige, in particular if they are working with underprivileged patients such as the old or the mentally ill.

If we look at the distribution of women within the medical profession, we find that 29 per cent of women doctors are GPs—about the right proportion in relation to their representation in the profession overall. However, women are under-represented amongst senior hospital doctors, particularly at the consultant level. Women are only 17 per cent of consultants. Within the consultant category, women are under-represented in the most prestigious specialties, and are only 4 per cent of surgeons (Allen 1994). Relatively speaking, however, women are over-represented in the less prestigious specialites. For example, 34 per cent of psychiatric specialists are women. It is clear, therefore, that although women have moved into the medical profession in increasing numbers, this is not reflected in their occupation of the most senior positions within medicine.

Many women who become doctors will no doubt choose particular jobs or specialities with a view to combining work and family life. Jobs in psychiatry, for example, have much more regular hours than jobs in surgery. Women are also over-represented in specialities such as radiology, where the hours are fairly regular, as well as in those reflecting the 'woman's role', such as paediatrics (specialists in children's medical care). It might be said that women doctors in such specialities have 'chosen' culturally feminine specialities, and/or medical jobs, that enable them to combine work and domesticity. However, there is also considerable evidence which demonstrates that male surgeons are often particularly hostile to women (Allen 1994). Examples of this hostility often has sexual overtones, as these quotations from recent research demonstrate: 'Women used to get reprimanded for wearing trousers, particularly in surgery . . . We had lectures where the lecturers used to put up slides of naked women in between the educational slides—just to keep the boys awake I think'; 'I've been treated badly by consultant surgeons. The nurse was off sick and he made me do her job rather than the two male doctors I was with' (p. 76).

As women have been gaining better educational qualifications, and the restrictions on their entry have been removed, so they have been moving into professional and managerial occupations (Crompton 1994; Crompton and Sanderson 1990). These changes in the levels of vertical occupational segregation are a significant development affecting the contemporary structure of women's employment (Hakim 1992). However, as we have seen, there are clear patterns of gender segregation *within* these higher-level occupations. Two factors associated with this internal re-segregation have been identified. First, particularly in the case of banking, the management structure into which women are gaining entry is itself in a process of transformation as a consequence of organizational restructuring. Thus women are not simply being 'slotted in' to stable and unchanging managerial jobs. In this fluid and ever-changing situation, gendered niches emerge within management itself, and women are concentrated in particular areas. Second, as we have seen in the case of the doctors, as women go into managerial and professional jobs, many will consciously choose areas which enable them to combine paid employment and domestic life.[9] Thus yet again, we can observe the interaction of choice and constraint in the structuring of women's employment.

It should not be forgotten, however, that for as long as the topmost occupational positions are male-dominated, male exclusionary practices are likely to remain important in keeping women out of these positions. These practices may not always be as extreme as the example of sexual harassment we examined in the last section. Nevertheless, they remain important, and the fact that they are so often associated with attempts at some kind of sexual domination suggests that they might be particularly difficult to change.

Summary and Conclusions: *Plus ça change, plus c'est la même chose?*

In this chapter we have reviewed the trends in and developments of the sociology of women and paid employment from the first reactions to the critiques of second-wave feminism, which tended to emphasize the *structural* factors shaping women's employment experiences, to more recent analyses which, reflecting recent theoretical developments within feminism itself, have emphasized, rather, the *processes* and *discourses* through which gender is constructed in employment.

This chapter has also provided a history of the recent changes in the employment situation of women. Here we used the banking industry (in particular the clearing banks) as a major example. This industry well illustrates the interaction between changes in the supply of and demand for women's labour. Here our emphasis remained upon the external and internal forces which have directly shaped both. That is, our explanation was broadly structural or materialist.

- Changes in the supply of women's labour are reflected in the broad changes in the position of women. Since the Second World War, married women have increasingly become available as a labour force as their childbearing patterns have changed. Legislation has made direct discrimination against women illegal. Women's educational levels have risen considerably and in many areas they now outstrip those of men. The impact of second-wave feminism has also had an impact on women's attitudes to paid work and equality (see Scott *et al.* 1996).

- Changes in demand take place because the employer's requirements are transformed. Technological change, in particular, has been very important in reshaping the nature of work. Much heavy and labour-intensive work can now be done by machines, and in traditional white-collar areas such as financial services the changes have been even more profound. Employers increasingly require a flexible labour force, and the kinds of qualities they are looking for in their workforce change as well.

We can better understand these requirements for particular kinds of employee qualities by moving beyond an approach which focuses upon supply and demand alone towards a *discourse* or *process* approach which emphasizes the active generation and reproduction of gendered occupations. Once the banks required solid, paternalistic men in their managerial jobs, particularly in branch banking. These requirements have shifted with the transformation of the industry, and now a 'competitive masculinity' and selling culture is encouraged. It was stressed, however, that much as these insights from this discursive, 'post-modern' approach to the study of employment might enhance our understanding of the pattern of women's employment, they do not *replace* material or structural explanations and interpretations.

Our analysis, therefore, continued to use a combined or multi-factor approach in our examination of sexual harassment. This was shown, firstly, to reflect a particularly aggressive, traditional kind of masculinity, and secondly, to be found more often when women are in 'non-traditional' occupations. This suggests that sexual harassment has a material as well as a sexual basis, in that 'non-traditional' occupations for women are usually better-paid. We therefore examined the recent entry of women into higher-level occupations.

Despite the decrease in vertical segregation—that is, women moving into occupations such as medicine and banking, which were previously dominated by men—we nevertheless find that internal re-segregation would seem to be taking place within the occupations in question. Within both medicine and bank management, women are over-represented in some areas, and under-represented in others: there are 'men's' jobs and 'women's' jobs. Our explanations of this re-segregation drew upon the whole range of the theoretical approaches, materialist and individualist, structural and processual, which have been developed to explain the patterning of women's (and men's) employment. This illustrates the value of a multidimensional, rather than a unidimensional, approach to the topic.

However, a major question still remains: despite all the changes which have taken place over the last twenty years, the gender contours of women's employment in Britain have not as yet been radically transformed. Does this mean that the more things change, the more they stay the same? We will be examining this question in Chapter 6, which will also return to a further consideration of some of the theoretical arguments discussed in this book.

Chapter Six

Discussion and Conclusions

Introduction

In this final chapter we will be bringing together the themes we have developed in this book under a number of headings. First, we will return to the major question posed in Chapter 1: how is the division of labour between men and women to be explained and understood? Our discussion will then move outwards, from a consideration of the topic of the gender division of labour in particular (broad though this is) to a discussion of the wider societal implications (for the family, and for social cohesion) of these contemporary changes and developments in the way in which different kinds of 'work' are distributed between men and women in Britain. Finally, we will briefly examine current debates as to the impact on *men* of changes in the nature of work and employment, and in the division of labour.

Explaining the Gender Division of Labour

This topic has only been seen as a legitimate object of enquiry since the fairly recent historical past. In traditional societies, the division of labour between men and women was viewed as largely 'natural'. Even with the transition to modern industrialism, we have seen that the ideology of 'separate spheres' of masculine and feminine activity, reflected in the division between market work and domestic work, persisted well into this century. Indeed, in many of the relatively more affluent societies in the West, the heyday of the 'male-breadwinner' model of the division of labour between the sexes might be seen as being during the period immediately after the Second World War. Relative affluence and increasing wage levels amongst the working class meant that the capacity to keep a wife (and children) at home extended further down into the social hierarchy than it had ever done previously.

The male-breadwinner model of the division of labour was reproduced by sociology in Parsons' (1949) functional theory of the modern family, in which the mother was the 'expressive leader' (that is, she was responsible for caring, emotion, and so on), and the husband/father was the 'instrumental leader' (that is, the breadwinner). In this structural functionalist approach, 'family' and 'economy' were viewed as distinct entities (or separate spheres), and the family was seen as carrying out specific functions (physical reproduction, nurturing) for the economy.

Once the division of labour between men and women was no longer seen as 'natural', and/or as following from the imperative demands of the family, it had to be explained. 'Second-wave' feminism, which developed from the 1960s onwards, was very important in developing this critique. Thus from the 1960s onwards it was argued that men had excluded women from the best jobs for their own advantage. Both Hartmann (1982) and Walby (1986) described this as an expression of patriarchy.[1] Men were seen as having developed institutions and structures which directly excluded women, in order both to gain material advantage for men as a whole and to secure the use of women's labour by individual men in the household. It was argued, however, that 'patriarchy' could not be used as a theory (that is, as a complete explanation of the situation of women). However, it is a useful term which describes men's subordination of women.

Recent history shows that women have, until fairly recently, been kept out (that is, excluded) from prestigious occupations such as medicine, from the 'best' universities such as Oxford and Cambridge, as well as from particular occupations such as printing and craft engineering. However, in most Western societies and in the ex-state-socialist regimes of Eastern Europe, these formal restrictions on women's participation have been removed. Nevertheless, even after their abolition, men's and women's employment still remains highly differentiated. Moreover, the relative hierarchy of men and women, male/female, in which men occupy the most powerful positions in work and society and women are subordinate, has not been transformed either. Feminists would argue that this is because men's power to exclude women from the better jobs has never rested in formal institutions alone, but also operates at the interpersonal level. As we saw in Chapter 5, men can, through sexual harassment in the workplace, directly exclude women from better jobs (although this practice is, of course, illegal). Others, however, have argued that too much emphasis has been placed upon structural factors in explaining women's employment patterns, and that, rather, it is the choices that women make that should be emphasized. Hakim (1996) is one of the most recent commentators to have argued this case.

However, throughout this book we have seen that both structural constraints *and* individual choices have to be taken into account in developing an explanatory account of the patterning of women's—and men's—paid employment. In Chapter 2, for example, we saw that whilst the majority of women who work part-time say that they would not want a full-time job, this finding has to be evaluated against a number of structural factors, including both the low level of childcare available in Britain, which means that women with caring responsibilities are likely to wish to work part-time (in Chapter 4, we saw that 30 per cent of employed mothers with children under 16 either worked at home or only worked during school hours), and also that changes in the wider economy mean that *employers* increasingly seek ('demand') flexible, part-time workers. That is, part-time work cannot simply be seen as being an expression of women's 'preferences'.

In Chapter 3, our cross-national comparisons demonstrated how important *national*, institutional structures are in shaping women's employment patterns. The way in which the welfare state has been developed has affected not only the extent of women's paid work, but also the manner in which it has been distributed. Some welfare states, particularly in the Scandinavian countries, have encouraged women's paid employment, and this employment is concentrated in the jobs created in the state-organized welfare sector. Other welfare states, such as Germany, have systems of taxation and welfare provision which discourage women's employment. Social insurance in Germany is organized on the assumption that women will be available to carry out caring work within the home, and thus the level of paid employment amongst women is lower.

Thus the *gender structuring* of paid employment has to be seen as an outcome of context, constraint, and choice. It is the outcome of what men and women, individually, as households, and collectively, do. However, what they *do* do changes over time. A good example of this kind of change in Britain would be the attitudes of trade unions towards women's paid employment. For most of this century, most trade unions in Britain supported the idea of the 'family wage'; that is, the idea that a wage should be sufficient to enable an employed man to support a wife and children (Barrett and Mackintosh 1980). This strategy saw employment for women as 'secondary', and indeed, trade unions have co-operated in the exclusion of women from particular areas of employment, as Hartmann and Walby have demonstrated. However, the situation is now transformed as trade unions give both the recruitment of female members and the promotion of equal opportunities policies a high priority.

Thus trade union policies towards women have changed in response to recent labour-market developments, in which the expansion of women's employment has been a major factor.[2] Changes in the structuring of paid employment, therefore, have had an impact upon the institutional context. However, the institutional context itself has often been originally formulated with reference to a particular state of affairs (or division of labour) which has been superseded. For example, as we saw in Chapter 3, most European welfare states were originally constructed on the assumption that the 'male-breadwinner' division of labour was predominant in society—as, indeed, it was after the Second World War, a crucial period in welfare-state development. This fact of historical change brings us to consider a further point which we emphasized in our introductory chapter. This is the essential interdependence of market and non-market (that is, household or domestic) 'work', even in a society such as our own, which is dominated by market relationships.

The Total Social Organization of Labour

A useful way of approaching the analysis of this interdependence is through Glucksmann's (1995) account of the Total Social Organization of Labour (TSOL), which was briefly discussed in Chapter 1. The TSOL is simply a description of how the totality of labour in any particular society is divided up between different institutions and activities. Thus the TSOL would be concerned with both the distribution of labour between different types of function (production, services, all types of welfare such as health and education), and the institutions (which could be factories, offices, households, voluntary organizations, or even labour camps) in which they are carried out. The market and the household economies of western industrial societies are two arenas within a larger structure of production and reproduction. 'What takes place in one is affected by and in turn affects the other . . . they are interdependent' (1995: 68).

Glucksmann, therefore, emphasizes the 'embeddedness' of 'work' in other activities and relationships, even in a society in which 'work' as employment is supposedly a separate, discrete area of activity. For example, as we saw in Chapter 5, stereotypical gender and sexual relationships are frequently carried over into workplace roles. 'Work' is defined by Glucksmann as an 'activity necessary for the production and reproduction of economic relations and structures in a particular Total Social Organization of Labour (TSOL), irrespective of how and where it is carried out' (1995: 69). Thus, for example, neither factory workers nor bureaucratic officials would be in a position to devote themselves full-time to their 'office' or employer if their basic domestic requirements were not met, and thus domestic work may be understood as 'work' in this TSOL context.

Glucksmann developed the TSOL concept in her analysis of historical changes in the distribution of men's and women's work in Britain. In the early years of industrial production, much production for use still took place within the household. Bread was baked, clothes made, food-stuffs preserved and stored. Thus a part of the wage brought into the household was used in order to purchase the raw materials for house-hold production. As we saw in Chapter 1, many households could not economically support all of their potential members. Domestic service, particularly for women, was very common; that is, women were paid a wage for carrying out domestic production in another household. Glucksmann argues that, during this period in which production was still to a considerable extent carried out within the household, women were simply not available, to any great extent, for waged work outside the household: 'Women could not be in two places at the same time: if they still had to bake bread, make clothes, boil up hot water, and pro-duce eleven children, they would not (be) available for waged work' (1995: 72). However, the development of mass production during the inter-war period relocated many women, particularly young women who would at one period would have been domestic servants, into waged (factory) work.

This movement of women into paid employment was associated with a decline in the birth-rate, which reduced the total amount of domestic work. However, domestic work still had to be done. This was in part achieved through the purchase of items that had previously been made in the household—clothes, processed food, and so on. It was also achieved through the introduction into the household of labour-saving devices such as vacuum cleaners, refrigerators, gas and electricity ovens and cookers, and washing machines. Women were recruited to mass production in large numbers in order to make consumer goods; their wages meant that households were enabled to buy them. The consumer goods expansion, however, was not (and could not have been) fuelled only by the increase in the total wages going into working-class house-holds. Most women still earned relatively low or 'component' (Siltanen 1986) wages only: that is, wages which were not of a level sufficient to support an independent household. Nevertheless, women who worked

Table 6.1 The 'male breadwinner' TSOL

	working-class	middle-class
men	main breadwinner	sole breadwinner
women	domestic work and/or 'component wage'	domestic work

in factories, shops, and offices were no longer available for domestic service. Glucksmann argues that many domestic tasks previously undertaken by servants were now done with the aid of labour-saving appliances, and 'amongst the new professional salariat the normal pattern was for wives to do their own housework, without residential servants, but aided by domestic machinery' (1995: 73). Thus the emergence of the middle-class housewife-manager was central to the TSOL of mass production.

Very schematically, Glucksmann's account of the TSOL in the era of mass production may be diagrammed as in Table 6.1.

There can be little doubt that, as far as many women were concerned, this model was inequitable. At a personal level, it often resulted in the frustration of individual hopes and ambitions, and at worst, the entrapment of women without other material supports in abusive relationships. Women without access to a 'breadwinner' were in a particularly vulnerable position. Yet as many commentators have noted, it did supply some kind of 'fit' between the household and the market economy, albeit at some (potential) expense to rather more than half the population. However, as we have seen in this book, circumstances are changing.

A New TSOL?—and its Consequences

As we have seen in Chapter 2, any account of the expansion of women's employment cannot be divorced from the wider changes that are taking place in the structure of employment as a whole. In brief, these are: the decline of employment in manufacturing industry and the shift to service employment; the growth of unemployment and long-term unemployment; and increasing employment flexibility. This would include both internal flexibility, that is, for example, the capacity to switch tasks or redeploy and retrain workers within the organization, as well as external flexibility, that is, the capacity to hire labour for specific periods, and to acquire and shed workers at will. As described in Chapter 2, the growth of external flexibility has resulted in an increase in part-time, sub-contract, consultancy, and short-term work, as well as the growth of self-employment (Beatson 1995a; b).

Technological change and the increasing speed-up of transactions brought about by developments such as computerized financial systems have certainly led to an increase in the demand for flexible workers. Consider, for example, the impact of the bar coding of prices of goods in supermarkets. Stock levels can be monitored as the shopper goes through the checkout, and new stocks ordered which will be delivered on the same day or overnight, from warehouses which are staffed around the clock. The constant monitoring of sales levels means that shop assistants called in in the morning may find themselves leaving work at midday if turnover is low—but at little or no cost to the employer, who has hired them at an hourly rate, or even from an employment agency. If the flow of customers increases, then an 'on-call' employee may be called in later in the day.

Since the end of the 1970s, government policies have served to encourage these kinds of labour-market trends. There has been a sustained effort to 'marketize' society, that is, to increase the extent to which 'the market' decides on the allocation of resources. In Britain industries such as gas, electricity, water, railways, and telephones have been sold to private owners. Housing which was once owned and rented out by local authorities (councils) has been sold to the tenants. Levels of direct taxation, particularly for the better off, have been reduced.[3] It is argued that this will encourage people to work harder in order to earn more. People are being encouraged to do the best for themselves as individuals. It is reasoned that, if an increasing number of individuals are successful, then the overall level of economic prosperity in the society as a whole will be raised as well.[4]

British society has not only been marketized and individualized, but the market, particularly the labour market, has been deregulated as well. The power and influence of trade unions has been drastically reduced. Job protections, such as Wages Councils, which used to set wage rates for the lowest-paid workers in industries such as clothing, have been removed. Employment flexibility has been encouraged. In fact, protective labour legislation in Britain has always been relatively weak and it has not been difficult for British employers to develop an increasingly flexible workforce. Flexibility has also increasingly begun to have an impact in areas which had previously been thought of as secure, such as administrative and managerial jobs. With increasing competition and marketization, firms and organizations are encouraged to 'downsize' (that is, employ fewer people), and to build 'lean organizations' (that is, employ fewer people). Thus organizations such as high-street banks, for example, are offering early retirement and making managerial staff redundant, something which was unheard of even fifteen years ago.

In this last chapter, we cannot begin to discuss the important question of whether the marketization of British society has or has not resulted in the development of a more successful economy. However, what would seem to be beyond dispute is that it has resulted in increasing social polarization and material inequality. Put simply, in a situation where there is increased competition and individualism, there are going to be losers as well as winners. The material gap between those at the bottom and those at the top has widened considerably. For example, the recent Rowntree Report (1995) showed that, between 1979 and 1991, whilst the income of the top 10 per cent rose by more than half, the real income of the bottom sixth of the population actually fell. Increasing inequality and rising unemployment have led some commentators to argue that Britain has become a '30: 30: 40' society (Hutton 1995: 14): 'Only around 40 per cent of the work-force enjoy tenured full-time employment or secure self-employment . . . , another 30 per cent are insecurely self-employed, involuntarily part-time, or casual workers; while the bottom 30 per cent, the marginalised, are idle or working for poverty wages'.

This '30: 30: 40' description has been used to describe the workforce, which is an aggregate of individuals. However, 'society' is made up of households (as well as other institutions), and not just individuals. Women's employment trends have intensified the widening inequalities within the workforce, as we have already noted in Chapter 4. These trends may be schematically mapped onto the 30: 30: 40 society to identify the likely types of couple-households associated with growing economic polarization,[5] as in Table 6.2.

Table 6.2 Employment and households in the 30: 30: 40 society

	30	30	40
men	unemployed	insecure full-time	full-time
women	unemployed	insecure part-time	full-time/part-time

All households, whether or not their members are in employment, will also have to undertake a certain amount of domestic labour. Those households whose members are in employment will, by definition, have less time available for domestic work. Thus the 30: 30: 40 society is one in which, increasingly, households are divided between those that have 'too much' work (the 40) and those that have 'too little' (the 30: 30) (Gorz 1989). The imbalance is intensified by the fact that people in work, particularly men, are tending to work longer hours. The not-very-well-paid (such as, for example, drivers and transport workers) have to work long hours in order to make up their wages. Managers in 'downsized' or 'lean' organizations may be concerned about their job security and work long hours in order to demonstrate their commitment to the job—a phenomenon that has been described as 'presentism'. A recent study showed that more than one in four fathers who are earning put in more than fifty hours a week at work, and almost one in ten work more than sixty hours a week (Ferri and Smith 1996).

Social polarization has also been accompanied by a growing concern about social order more generally. Crime levels (particularly theft of property) are increasing, especially amongst young people; the number of pupils excluded from school is growing; and permanent unemployment amongst young people would seem to be associated with a whole range of anti-social behaviour. The rising level of concern about young people has led to something approaching a moral panic about the erosion of conventional family life and a supposed 'parenting deficit'. One reaction to these trends has been to argue for a return to traditional family values, including the reinforcement of the woman's (mother's) role in domesticity and parenting. It has also been suggested that, because of a lack of suitable role models, young people should be offered classes in parenting, and indeed, that these classes should be made compulsory for some categories of family.

It may seem paradoxical, but very often those people who advocate parenting classes and women's return to the home are the same ones as those who emphasize the values of individualism and the virtues of a deregulated, marketized society, which has encouraged the development of the kinds of jobs with incomes insufficient to support households. It is true that European comparisons show that countries like Britain (and the United States, which has pursued similar policies), have created proportionately *more* jobs (in part) as a result of such policies, but the problem is that they also tend to be *poor* jobs. Women tend to predominate in less well-paid, flexible employment. A recent survey of employment trends (Royal Society of Arts, *Towards a New*

Definition of Work, 1996) suggests an inescapable logic. The first five points identified were:

- *fewer full-time jobs*: down 207,000 net since 1984; less than 60 per cent of the workforce and declining.
- *fewer male full-time jobs*: down 807,000 since 1984; female full-time up 600,000.
- *more part-time jobs*: now 28 per cent of all jobs; doubled since 1971, up 2.6 m to 6.1 m; set to grow by 1.3 m jobs by the year 2000.
- *more women part-time employees*: 45 per cent of women in employment now work part-time.
- *new jobs*: Between 80 and 90 per cent will go to women.

These predictions suggest that the jobs which are being created at the present time are not the kinds of jobs which would allow for a return to the 'male-breadwinner' model of employment and family life, even if men and women wished to achieve this end. Is social polarization, therefore, an inevitable outcome of current trends in employment, of which the expansion of 'women's work' is just a part? It may be argued that it is not.

Much of the flexibilization of employment has come about because of underlying changes in the organization of production, distribution, and exchange, as well as changes in social attitudes and norms. However, these changes did not take place in a vacuum. We have argued above that the marketization of British society and the flexibilization of employment is also in large part the outcome of government policies which have encouraged individualism and competition. In such an environment, neither people nor organizations are encouraged to take a wider view. If a cheap and flexible labour force gives a competitive edge, then employers may not judge it sensible to invest in training or employment benefits for their workers (which might make them feel more secure and motivated). People with insecure and/or poorly paid jobs find it difficult to obtain mortgages for housing, and/or set up families. Thus Hutton (1995: 225) argues that, 'a market society takes a terrible toll of the social groupings that represent the building blocks of our humanity—from the parenting of our children to the reliability of public transport'.

This is a book about sociology, not politics. However, in the light of the evidence we have reviewed in this book, it might be suggested that in respect of the paid employment and family/household interface, alternative policies could be adopted which might help to ameliorate social polarization. Commonsensically, it would seem useful to be able to redistribute work from households which have 'too much' work to households which have 'too little'. Here it will be helpful to extend the reasoning behind the TSOL to present circumstances. If women are engaging in more paid work then, given that they have traditionally carried out domestic work and caring, a part of this work will have to be achieved by other means. Women can intensify their work (the 'double burden'), and/or men can do more of this kind of work. However, the increasing participation of women in paid work is also likely to result in some kind of job creation, from take-away meals to crèches and retirement homes. Many of these jobs will be poorly paid: indeed, this is one reason why such jobs have been considered to be 'women's work'. However, this does not have to be the case. For example, jobs, (including flexible jobs) could be given an increased level of social protections as compared to those which prevail at the moment. These would include holiday entitlements, the regulation of working hours, and other employment-related benefits such as sick pay and pension schemes. Jobs could also be made more 'family-friendly'. Paternity leave, leave to care for sick family members, workplace nurseries, and so on are all measures which would make family life easier. This would involve a degree of labour-market direction and regulation which some would say was 'uneconomic'. However, a recent report suggests that companies which do make this kind of provision for their workers are in general more profitable than those which do not.[6]

Thus, the TOSL would be adapted to current trends. In part, this would be reflected in the improvements in job conditions being argued for above. A company which was genuinely concerned with its employees' welfare, for example, would probably not want the parents of young children, or other carers, to work excessively long hours. The provision of good and well-regulated childcare and eldercare could create good jobs rather than 'junk jobs'. Caring itself involves qualities and skills which are extremely valuable—indeed, essential—to society as a whole, but which do not necessarily demand the intensive development of academic and technical skills. There is no reason why men should not do these jobs as well as women. Properly regulated and organized, the work of caring could become a source of good employment.

These kinds of development would help to achieve some kind of balance between the fact of rising female employment and family life. Such a scenario might be dismissed as unduly optimistic. Not only might there be considerable opposition from politicians and the business community to these kinds of changes, but men (and possibly women) themselves might be unwilling to make the personal changes that might be involved.

Men's Troubles

In recent years the circumstances of men have been seen as becoming increasingly problematic. Men lower down the social scale have increasingly found themselves without jobs, and it is being argued that, higher up the social scale, men are finding it difficult to adapt to the new realities of flexible employment. Girls have not only caught up with boys in respect of formal educational qualifications, but have begun to overtake them. Girls are more successful than boys at every level in GCSE, with more achieving at least one grade G and more passing in at least five subjects at grade C or above. Increasingly, schools are being urged to focus upon low-achieving boys, and the low-achieving, unskilled male is seen as an intractable social problem.

It may be suggested that this is, at least in part, a consequence of the lack of job opportunities for young, unskilled males. If few opportunities are seen to be available, then the incentive to gain qualifications will be reduced and a vicious spiral instituted. 'Traditional' male working-class jobs, requiring physical strength but not usually thought of as 'skilled', have disappeared in large numbers. Whole communities have been devastated as mines, steelworks, shipbuilding yards, docks, and other heavy industries have either closed altogether or been subject to massive rationalization and technical change, with a great loss of men's jobs.

The problems of working-class men are most pressing and immediate, but it has also been argued that even 'successful' men are having difficulties in making adjustments to the changing world of paid employment. For example, Pahl (1995) has argued that the separation of spheres between domestic work and paid work (and thus women and men) may ultimately prove to have been more of a handicap to men than women. Following Siedler's (1987) analysis of masculinity, Pahl argues that from the eighteenth and nineteenth centuries, developments of masculine rationality and engagement with the outside world—as embodied in the captain of industry, the colonial expansionist, the frontier settler, and so on—had the effect of making men learn to repress emotions and cut themselves off from their own feelings. 'Real men' were taught to exercise emotional control, and the separation of spheres left the emotional work to women. Modern masculinity, Pahl argues, was also built upon the model of the male as provider: 'the idea that men sacrifice themselves or "do it all for their families" has done much to develop a distinctive model of masculinity' (1995: 190). In order to achieve success in the market, men are also forced to seek power: 'part of being masculine is to seek and hold power, to be in control and to favour action as a way of coping in the outside competitive world' (ibid.).

As emotionally controlled, power-seeking providers, Pahl argues, men are ill-prepared for the workplace and family flexibilities that are increasingly required today. Men's emotional reticence makes it difficult for them to relate to their children and grandchildren. It also makes it difficult for them to adapt to the more interactive demands of the new, people-related jobs in customer-oriented service industries. Men's embrace of the provider role and commitment to success in the marketplace means that their masculinity will be undermined if this provider role disappears, and/or they find themselves having to change (or even losing) their jobs in mid-career. In contrast, women have a greater capacity to be flexible. However, this makes men even more vulnerable, and 'it may well be that most men experience women's growing success in all spheres as a kind of threat they are reluctant to acknowledge' (1995: 191). However, in general men are 'receiving very little support and understanding for the changes they are forced to undergo' (1995: 194).

It is true that the pace of social change since the mid-twentieth century has been extremely rapid for both men and women. However, it would be difficult to argue that the problems they have brought have been excessively difficult for men in particular. As we have seen in Chapter 5, men still retain their predominance in the world of paid work, and we should be cautious of assuming that the 'deposing of the centrality of the male from the sphere of employment' (Pahl 1995: 191) has in fact taken place. It is also important to recognize that the kind of emotionally controlled, power-seeking masculinity that Pahl describes is in any case characteristic of a particular kind of masculinity, in particular one which is white, European, and middle-class. As Connell (1995) has argued, there are extensive class and ethnic differences in masculinities, and homosexual as well as heterosexual masculinities may be developed. Thus a challenge to the particular kind of masculinity described by Pahl (if, indeed, it is taking place) does not necessarily mean that all men are vulnerable or under threat. Indeed, it might be suggested that the contestation or modification of the power-seeking, competitive, emotionally depthless, provider-model of masculinity might be of some advantage to men and women alike. Pahl himself would seem to be suggesting this when he argues for the need to move towards a more balanced, and less power-dominated, version of 'success'.

Rather more negatively, there have been a number of other signs of a

'backlash' against the kinds of gains that women have achieved in relation to men, even though the evidence of this book suggests that these
gains are rather modest (Faludi 1992). Sometimes this backlash is quite
straightforward, as in references to 'that group of highly educated and
professional feminists who have benefited so much from equal opportunities measures. They have positions that often give them time to
have it all and money to pay other women to look after the kids' (*The
Higher*, 15 November 1996). Such statements reflect a fairly un-
varnished resentment of some women's success. Other strands, such as
the men's therapy movement, are more subtle, but are nevertheless not
particularly well disposed towards women's equality. For example,
Bly's (1990) influential book, *Iron John*, argues that men have to recover
the 'deep masculine' that lies within themselves which they have been
forced to repress. Masculinity therapy (usually paid for by white,
middle-class males) seeks to recover the masculine in men-only
therapy sessions involving drumming, pretending to be warriors (that
is, stereotypical tribal 'men'), and so on. The men's therapy movement
may be seen as developing a stronger version of the kinds of arguments
developed by Pahl concerning the damage that has been done to men in
the modern world of increasing female assertiveness and economic
participation. There is a preoccupation with men's emotional wounds
and need for personal healing which, by describing men as victims,
effectively glosses over the continuing extent of material differences
between men and women.

However, it may be argued that, rather than attempting to recast men
as victims of the kinds of social changes associated with changes in the
gender division of labour, it is more appropriate to move beyond the
oppositional gender stance implied in these commentaries. Both men
and women may suffer emotional damage of one kind or another; both
men and women will experience the difficulties associated with poverty, joblessness, and rising inequality. Nevertheless, a complete identity (or androgyny) in the division of all kinds of work between men and
women is not ever likely to be a reality. (Androgyny refers to the notion
that men and women should be the same in every respect.) Men and
women are different from each other; and differences may be positive
as well as negative. Nevertheless, these differences (besides the obvious
biological differences, we should also include socially constructed differences in matters such as felt responsibility for childcare and domestic tasks, in willingness to use violence to achieve ends, or to make
sacrifices for a career) mean that it is unlikely that absolute material
equality between the sexes, on an individual basis, will ever be a reality.
Furthermore, as Connell has argued, 'the general interest of men in

patriarchy is formidable' (1995: 241).[7] As we have seen in our discussion of sexual harassment in Chapter 5, men are also capable of acting directly in order to secure this interest. It is still largely men that hold political and economic power, and control the means of violence. This rests, in part, upon the nature of the division of labour between men and women.

Summary and Conclusions

Nevertheless, on the basis of the empirical evidence in this book, and the arguments that have been developed in this and other chapters, it may be argued that both in Britain, and in other similar European and European-influenced countries, we may anticipate a continued blurring of the stereotypical boundaries characteristic of the gender division of labour.

- Although some sex-typing of household tasks is likely to continue, the increase in the amount of domestic work carried out by men is a trend which is likely to persist. Men do most domestic work when their wives are in full-time employment, and more and more women are working full-time, even when they have small children. In any case, Gershuny *et al.*'s (1994) data show that the amount of domestic work carried out by men has shown a small but steady increase over time, even when wives are not in employment, or only working part-time.

- More women are moving into managerial and professional occupations (the fastest-growing occupational category), and this trend shows no sign of slackening. It is true that women tend to be located in 'gendered niches' within managerial and professional occupations. Nevertheless, such jobs will usually generate an income which is sufficient to live independently. Managerial and professional women are likely to enter into relationships with men in occupations at a similar level, and to remain in paid employment after the birth of their children. Such households will require various services which will have to be purchased, either directly through the employment of paid domestic help, or indirectly through ready-made meals, restaurants, dry cleaners, and so on. More generally, two-earner households (that is, not only managerial and professional) will be more likely to buy services of all kinds.

- More men will take up the employment thus created. That is, there will be an increasing move of men into service occupations, thus further blurring the boundaries of the gender division of labour in the sphere of paid employment. In Chapter 2 we saw that between 1979 and 1990 more men have taken up catering, cleaning, and other personal service occupations, as well as professional and related jobs in education, welfare, and health (Table 2.1). Indeed, detailed analyses of recent employment data show that 'care assistant' was one of the single most rapidly growing occupations for men. There is nothing intrinsically 'feminine' about such jobs, and no obvious reason why they should be poorly paid. In this final chapter it has been argued that job upgrading and regulation would benefit not only the women and men employed in such occupations, but would also make a contribution to a reduction of the level of material and social polarization in British society.

In conclusion, therefore, there are some grounds for a guarded optimism as far as movement towards a less rigid division of labour between the sexes is concerned, in respect of both paid and unpaid work. Attitudes are changing as well. A recent survey, for example, shows that in Britain the proportion of interviewees disagreeing with the statement, 'A husband's job is to earn money, a wife's job is to look after the home and family' (that is, rejecting stereotypical gender roles) had increased from 53 per cent to 59 per cent between 1988 and 1994, and similar trends were noted in other countries (Scott *et al.* 1996). In his work on masculinity, Connell (1995: 226) describes 'a young working-class man with a record of violence, unemployment and imprisonment, briskly endorsing equal rights for women and complaining about "prejudiced blokes" who do not'. Connell continues, 'The vast change in legitimation over the past century is, for me, summed up in that comment.'

However, to return again to the analytical themes developed in Chapter 1, these attitudinal changes have not developed in thin air, but within an environment in which women as a whole have been making steady improvements in their *material* situations. Changes in attitudes to women and women's employment, which are themselves reflective of the development of different discourses of masculinity and femininity, have taken place against a 'lived experience' in which 'material structures and relationships' (Maynard 1995) are changing as well. A degree of internal resegregation may be taking place within higher-level managerial and professional occupations, but it is not absolute. In any case, even jobs in the 'feminized niches' within such occupations generate sufficient income for independent living. The more income a woman brings into a household, the more likely she is to share decision-making within the household, and the more likely is her partner to do a greater share of domestic work (Chapter 4). In short, it should always be borne in mind that, although changes in both attitudes to women and paid employment, and ideologies and discourses of masculinity and femininity, are certainly very important, it is improvements in the material situation of women relative to men which are most likely to secure their equal treatment within society.

Notes

Notes to Chapter One

1. Critiques of Humphries may be found in Walby (1986) and Barrett and Mackintosh (1980). An excellent review of the historical debate is to be found in Bradley (1989). For a contrary view, see Pahl (1988).
2. Developments in social theory have had a similar impact in other key sociological areas, such as debates around the concept of 'class'. See Crompton (1993).

Notes to Chapter Two

1. An early study (Hakim 1987) came up with the surprising finding that the level of homeworking amongst ethnic minority women was very low. However, Felstead and Jewson (1996) have demonstrated that Hakim's procedures and estimates were unreliable as far as ethnic minority homeworkers were concerned.
2. In the 1960s and 1970s there was a debate in sociology about 'orientations to work' which was centrally concerned with just these issues. It showed that whilst men might be content with one aspect of their job—such as pay—they could nevertheless be very critical of other aspects, such as job content. For a discussion of this topic and its relation to Hakim's arguments, see Crompton and Harris forthcoming.
3. Although, as we shall see in Chapter 3, there are countries, particularly in Scandinavia, with relatively high levels of occupational segregation but smaller wage gaps than countries with higher levels of segregation.
4. Indeed, for most of this century, for men (but not for women), 'clerk' was seen as a position on a ladder of promotion, rather than a final destination.

Notes to Chapter Three

1. The term 'fordist' is derived from the name of Henry Ford. He founded the Ford car company, and is widely credited with having played a central role in the development of standardized mass-manufacturing production. Societies dominated by mass-manufacturing industry have been described as 'fordist', and the high point of this period is argued to have been from the end of the Second World War until the end of the 1960s. The terms 'post-industrial',

'post-fordist', and 'post-modernist' have all been used to indicate a broad sweep of changes which would include the growth of services, the restructuring of social relationships, and increasing social fragmentation. As Esping-Andersen is concerned with the implication of the decline of manufacturing, his use of the term 'post-industrial' is appropriate here.

2. It should be noted that, at the moment, the Swedish Welfare State is in the process of being 'rolled back' and marketized. This has not happened, however, in the case of Norway, which is the example we use in this chapter.

3. It must be stressed that Esping-Andersen's argument is extremely complex and grounded in a wealth of empirical data, and it has been possible to give only a very oversimplified version here.

4. The Czech Republic was formed out of the division of Czechoslovakia into the Czech Republic and Slovenia, which took place at the end of 1994. The most recent data given is for the Czech Republic, but much of the information given here relates to the 'Czechoslovakian' period.

5. In Walby's terms, it might be argued that 'private patriarchy' persisted in France until the 1960s!

6. The level of part-time work is very low in the Czech Republic. In the state socialist era, everybody worked full-time, and this is still reflected in the contemporary figures. Officially there was also no unemployment. However, in this situation of over-employment there was also quite a lot of *de facto* flexibility as far as working hours were concerned (for both men and women). Women with young children, for example, would be allowed to leave early to collect them from school, or take time off if they were ill.

Notes to Chapter Four

1. Social and Community Planning Research (London) kindly gave access to this data.

2. See the discussion of 'work' on p. 15, Ch. 1.

3. Nevertheless, it should be remembered that Gershuny's study suggests that the extent of domestic work amongst husbands in rising even in households where women are not in employment.

4. See page 16.

Notes to Chapter Five

1. The Hawthorne studies have been widely criticized on other grounds as well. The improvements in productivity might be explained by the system of material incentives introduced. For example, the 'team leader', who encouraged higher productivity at all costs, became the sole supporter of her family during the period of the research.

2. Employment opportunities in the finance sector have been sharply reduced over the last few years, but for most of the period this assumption holds good.

3. The 'clearing' banks are so called because they co-operated in the nightly 'clearing' of all transactions—cheques—in London in the pre-mechanization era.

4. As they rose through the ranks, young clerks were 'tiered' in respect of their managerial suitability, and in consequence, a number not seen as suitable would leave 'voluntarily' at a relatively young age.

5. It is not being argued that exclusionary practices have disappeared altogether, but rather, that they are no longer required to the same extent.

6. This position is often referred to as 'post-structuralist'. For a discussion of the concept see Giddens (1987).

7. For example, bank managers were expected to be not only respectable but married, and would not usually get promotion unless they were married. This was reflected in enhanced pay scales for married men which persisted until the 1960s.

8. The figures quoted here were supplied by a major clearing bank that prefers to remain anonymous.

9. The example used here has been medicine, but the same pattern is also found in other professions. See, for example, Evett's work on engineers (1995), as well as Devine (1992).

Notes to Chapter Six

1. The insight was by no means original. As we saw in Chapter 1, earlier feminists such as Alice Clarke and Ivy Pinchbeck had also developed these arguments.

2. There have, of course, been many other factors affecting trade union behaviour, not least the hostile political climate in which they have existed since the end of the 1970s, and the legislation to curb their activities which has accompanied it.

3. Direct taxation is taxation of earned income and this has been reduced. Indirect taxation refers to taxes on corporations and commodities—for example, on fuel, cigarettes, and alcohol, and Value Added Tax (VAT), which is levied on a wide range of goods and services. The level of indirect taxes has not been reduced. As the less well-off tend to spend more of their income on commodities, they will frequently end up spending a greater proportion of their income in tax than the better off.

4. Pensions, and other aspects of old-age provision, have also been privatized. This may be described as the marketizing of social insurance. Relatively speaking, the value of the basic state pension has been brought down, and the government has encouraged people to make their own pension arrangements. Again, the emphasis is upon the importance of the individual taking upon themselves the responsibility for their own self-provision. (One by-product of these changes has been to further expand the financial services sector.) Thus there has been an effort to reduce the level of state employment,

not only by selling off industries and services which were once state owned or controlled, but also by reducing the level of services provided by the state in areas such as pensions provision. In areas in which state provision is still extensive, such as health, an internal market has been introduced.

5. As we have seen in Chapter 4, single-parent households, whether male or female headed, are likely to be unemployed households.

6. Kleinwort Benson have developed an investment methodology which identifies those companies adopting an 'inclusive' approach to management and development, one which includes both long-term investment and enhanced employment rights for workers. Their analysis suggests that 'inclusive' companies perform better than others. See *Tomorrow's Company* (London: RSA 1995).

7. Connell (1995) develops a series of arguments and suggestions concerning the possibilities of undermining and opposing patriarchal structures, but this is not our main concern here.

LIVERPOOL
JOHN MOORES UNIVERSITY
AVRIL ROBARTS LRC
TITHEBARN STREET
LIVERPOOL L2 2ER
TEL. 0151 231 4022

References

ACKER, J., and VAN HOUTEN, D. R. (1974), 'Differential Recruitment and Control: The Sex Structuring of Organisations', *Administrative Science Quarterly*, 14(1): 152–63.

ALLEN, S., and WOLKOWITZ, C. (1987), *Homeworking: Myths and Realities* (London: Macmillan Education).

ALLEN, I. (1994), *Doctors and their Careers* (London: Policy Studies Institute).

ARBER, S., and GINN, J. (1995), 'Gender Difference in the Relationship between Paid Work and Informal Care', *Work, Employment and Society*, 9(3): 445–71.

BANKS, O. (1981), *Faces of Feminism* (Oxford: Martin Robertson).

BARRETT, M., and MACKINTOSH, M. (1980), 'The "Family Wage"', *Capital and Class* (Summer), 51–72.

BARRETT, M. (1987), 'The Concept of "Difference"', *Feminist Review*, 26: 35–47.

BEATSON, M. (1995*a*), 'Progress Towards a Flexible Labour Market', *Employment Gazette* (February), 55–66.

—— (1995*b*), *Labour Market Flexibility* (London: Department of Employment).

BECK, U. (1992), *Risk Society* (London: Sage).

—— and BECK-GERNSHEIM, E. (1995), *The Normal Chaos of Love* (Cambridge: Polity).

BECKER, G. S. (1985), 'Human Capital, Effort, and the Sexual Division of Labour', *Journal of Labour Economics*, 3: 533–58.

BEECHEY, V., and PERKINS, T. (1987), *A Matter of Hours* (Cambridge: Polity).

BEVERIDGE, W. H. (1942), *Social Insurance and Allied Services* (HMSO Cmnd. 6404).

BLY, R. (1990), *Iron John* (Reading, Mass.: Addison-Wesley).

BOTT, E. (1957), *Family and Social Network* (London: Tavistock).

BRADLEY, H. (1989), *Men's Work, Women's Work* (Cambridge: Polity).

—— (1996), *Fractured Identities* (Cambridge: Polity).

BRAVERMAN, H. (1974), *Labor and Monopoly Capital* (New York: Monthly Review Press).

BROWN, R. (1976), 'Women as Employees', in S. Allen and D. L. Barker (eds.), *Dependence and Exploitation in Work and Marriage* (London: Longman).

BRUEGEL, I. (1996), 'Whose Myths are they Anyway?' *British Journal of Sociology*, 47(1): 175–7.

BUCKLEY, M. (1989), *Women and Ideology in the Soviet Union* (Hemel Hempstead: Harvester Wheatsheaf).

CAPLOW, T. (1954), *The Sociology of Work* (New York: McGraw-Hill).

CHANDLER, J., BRYANT, L., and BUNYARD, T. (1995), 'Women in Military Occupations', *Work, Employment and Society*, 9(1): 123–35.

CHODOROW, N. (1978), *The Reproduction of Mothering* (Berkeley: Univ. of

Calfornia Press).

CHODOROW, N. (1989), *Psychoanalysis and Feminism* (New Haven and London: Yale University Press).

CLARK, A. (1982), *Working Life of Women in the Seventeenth Century* (London: Routledge).

CMND (1988) 849 (London: HMSO).

COCKBURN, C. (1983), *Brothers: Male Dominance and Technological Change* (London: Pluto Press).

—— (1991), *In the Way of Women* (Basingstoke: Macmillan).

COHEN, B. (1988), *Caring for Children: Services and Policies for Childcare and Equal Opportunities in the UK* (London: Commission of the European Communities).

—— (1990), *Caring for Children: The 1990 Report* (Edinburgh: Scottish Child and Family Alliance).

COLLINSON, M., and COLLINSON, D. (1996), 'It's Only Dick: The Sexual Harassment of Women Managers in Insurance Sales', *Work, Employment and Society*, 10(1): 29–56.

CONNELL, R. W. (1995), *Masculinities* (Cambridge: Polity).

COYLE, A. (1982), 'Sex and Skill in the Organisation of the Clothing Industry', in J. West (ed.), *Women, Work and the Labour Market* (London: Routledge).

CRAIB, I. (1987), 'Masculinity and Male Dominance', *Sociological Review*, 721–43.

CROMPTON, R., and MANN, M. (eds.) (1985; 1994 edn.) *Gender and Stratification* (Cambridge: Polity).

CROMPTON, R. (1988), 'The Feminisation of the Clerical Labour Force since the Second World War', in G. Anderson (ed.), *The White-Blouse Revolution* (Manchester: Manchester University Press).

—— (1992), 'Where did all the Bright Girls Go?', in N. Abercrombie and A. Warde (eds.), *Social Change in Modern Britain* (Cambridge: Polity).

—— (1993), *Class and Stratification* (Cambridge: Polity).

—— (1994), 'Occupational Trends and Women's Employment Patterns', in R. Lindley (1994).

—— and JONES, G. (1984), *White-Collar Proletariat: Deskilling and Gender in the Clerical Labour Process* (London: Macmillan).

CROMPTON, R., and SANDERSON, K. (1986), 'Credentials and Careers', *Sociology*, 20(1): 25–42.

—— (1990), *Gendered Jobs and Social Change* (London: Unwin Hyman).

—— (1994), 'The Gendered Restructuring of Employment in the Finance Sector', in A. MacEwen Scott (ed.), *Gender Segregation and Social Change* (Oxford: Oxford University Press).

CROMPTON, R., GALLIE, D., and PURCELL, K. (eds.) (1996), *Changing Forms of Employment* (London: Routledge).

CROMPTON, R. (1989), 'Women in Banking', *Work, Employment and Society*, 3(2): 141–56.

—— and LE FEUVRE, N. (1992), 'Gender and Bureaucracy: Women in Finance in Britain and France', *Sociological Review Monograph*, ed. M. Savage and A. Witz

(Oxford: Blackwell).

—— (1996), 'Paid Employment and the Changing System of Gender Relations: A Cross-National Comparison', *Sociology*, 30(3): 427–45.

CROMPTON, R., and HARRIS, F. (forthcoming), 'Explaining Women's Employment Patterns: "Orientations to Work" Revisited', *British Journal of Sociology*.

DAHRENDORF, R. (1969), 'On the Origin of Inequality Among Men', in A. Beteille (ed.), *Social Inequality* (Harmondsworth, Middlesex: Penguin).

DAVIDOFF, L., and HALL, C. (1987), *Family Fortunes* (London: Hutchinson).

DENNIS, N., HENRIQUES, F., and SLAUGHTER, C. (1969), *Coal is our Life* (London: Tavistock).

DEVINE, F. (1992), 'Gender Segregation in the Engineering and Science Professions', *Work Employment and Society*, 6: 557–75.

DiTOMASO, N. (1989), 'Sexuality in the Workplace: Discrimination and Harrassment', in Hearn *et al.* (1989).

ELLINGSAETER, A. L. (1992), *Part-Time Work in European Welfare States* (Report 92 : 10 ISF Oslo).

ELSON, D. (ed.) (1991), *Male Bias in the Development Process* (Manchester: Manchester University Press).

ENGELS, F. (1940), *The Origins of the Family, Private Property, and the State* (London: Lawrence and Wishart).

ESPING-ANDERSEN, G. (1990), *The Three Worlds of Welfare Capitalism* (Cambridge: Polity).

—— (ed.) (1993), *Changing Classes: Stratification and Mobility in Post-Industrial Societies* (London: Sage).

EU (1992; 1995) *Bulletin on Women and Employment in the EU.*

EUROPEAN COMMISSION (1992), *Bulletin on Women and Employment* (October).

EVETTS, J. (1994), 'Women and Careers in Engineering', *Work Employment and Society*, 8: 101–12.

FALUDI, S. (1992), *Backlash* (London: Vintage).

FELDBERG, R. L., and GLENN, E. N. (1979), 'Male and Female: Job versus Gender Models in the Sociology of Work', *Social Problems*, 26(5): 524–38.

FELSTEAD, A., and JEWSON, N. (1996), 'Researching a Problematic Concept: Homeworkers in Britain', *University of Leicester Discussion Papers in Sociology*, no. S96/4.

FERRI, E., and SMITH, K. (1996), *Parenting in the 1990s* (London: Family Policy Studies Centre).

FINLAYSON, L. R., FORD, R., and MARSH, A. (1996), 'Paying More for Child Care', *Employment Gazette* (July), 295–303.

FRIEDAN, B. (1965), *The Feminine Mystique* (Harmondsworth: Penguin).

GAME, A., and PRINGLE, R. (1984), *Gender at Work* (London: Pluto Press).

GERSHUNY, J., GODWIN, M., and JONES, S. (1994), 'The Domestic Labour Revolution: A Process of Lagged Adaptation', in M. Anderson, F. Bechhofer, and J. Gershuny (eds.), *The Social and Political Economy of the Household* (Oxford: Oxford University Press).

GIDDENS, A. (1991), *Modernity and Self Identity* (Cambridge: Polity).

—— (1992), *The Transformation of Intimacy* (Cambridge: Polity).

References

GINN, J., ARBER, S., BRANNEN, J., DALE, A., DEX, S., ELIAS, P., MOSS, P., PAHL, J., ROBERTS, C., RUBERY, J. (1996), 'Feminist Fallacies: A Reply to Hakim on Women's Employment', *British Journal of Sociology*, 7(1): 167–74.

GLUCKSMANN, M. (1990), *Women Assemble* (London: Routledge).

——(1995), 'Why "work"? Gender and the "Total Social Organisation of Labour"', *Gender, Work and Organisation*, 2(2): 63–75.

GOLDTHORPE, J. H., LOCKWOOD, D., BECHHOFER, F., and PLATT, J. (1968), *The Affluent Worker: Industrial Attitudes and Behaviour* (Cambridge: Cambridge University Press).

——(1969), *The Affluent Worker in the Class Structure* (Cambridge: Cambridge University Press).

GORZ, A. (1989), *Critique of Economic Reason* (London: Verso).

GOULDNER, A. (1954), *Patterns of Industrial Bureaucracy* (New York: The Free Press).

GREGSON, N., and LOWE, M. (1994), *Servicing the Middle Classes* (London: Routledge).

GUTEK, B. A. (1989), 'Sexuality in the Workplace: Key Issues in Social Research and Organisational Practice', in Hearn *et al.* (1989).

HAKIM, C. (1979), *Occupational Segregation* (Department of Employment, Research Paper no. 9).

——(1991), 'Grateful Slaves and Self-Made Women: Fact and Fantasy in Women's Work Orientations', *European Sociological Review*, 7(2): 101–21.

——(1992), 'Explaining Trends in Occupational Segregation: The Measurement, Causes, and Consequences of the Sexual Division of Labour', *European Sociological Review*, 8(2): 127–52.

——(1995), 'Five Feminist Myths about Women's Employment', *British Journal of Sociology*, 46(3): 429–55.

——(1996), *Key Issues in Women's Work* (London: Athlone Press).

HALFORD, S., and SAVAGE, M. (1995), 'Restructuring Organisations, Changing People', *Work, Employment and Society*, 9(1): 97–122.

HALSEY, A. H. (1988), *British Social Trends since 1900* (London: Macmillan).

HANTRAIS, L. (1993), 'Women, Work and Welfare in France', in J. Lewis (ed.) (1993).

——(1990), *Managing Professional and Family Life: A Comparative Study of British and French Women* (Aldershot: Dartmouth).

HARROP, A., and MOSS, P. (1994), 'Working Parents: Trends in the 1980s', *Employment Gazette* (October), 343–51.

HARTMANN, H. (1981), 'The Unhappy Marriage of Marxism and Feminism: Towards a More Progressive Union', in L. Sargent (ed.), *Women and Revolution* (London: Pluto Press).

——(1982), 'Capitalism, Patriarchy and Job Segregation by Sex', reprinted in A. Giddens and D. Held (eds.), *Classes, Power and Conflict* (London and Basingstoke: Macmillan).

HEARN, J., SHEPPARD, D. L., TANCRED-SHERIFF, P., and BURRELL, G. (eds.) (1989), *The Sexuality of Organization* (London: Sage).

HEITLINGER, A. (1979), *Women and State Socialism* (London: Macmillan).

HERNES, H. (1987), *Welfare State and Woman Power* (Oslo: Norwegian University Press).

HOCHSCHILD, A. (1990), *The Second Shift* (London: Piatkus).

HUMPHRIES, J. (1984), in R. Pahl (ed.), *Divisions of Labour* (Oxford: Basil Blackwell).

—— (1982), 'Class Struggle and the Persistence of the Working-Class Family', in A. Giddens and D. Held (eds.), *Classes, Power and Conflict* (Basingstoke: Macmillan).

HUTTON, W. (1995), *The State We're In* (London: Jonathan Cape).

JENSON, J. (1986), 'Gender and Reproduction', *Studies in Political Economy*, 20: 9–46.

——, HAGEN, E., and REDDY, C. (eds.) (1988), *Feminization of the Labour Force: Paradoxes and Promises* (New York: Oxford University Press).

JOSEPH ROWNTREE FOUNDATION (1995), *Inquiry into Income and Wealth* (York).

KANTER, R. M. (1977), *Men and Women of the Corporation* (New York: Basic Books).

KOLBERG, J. E., and KOLSTAD, A. (1993), 'The Post-Industrial Stratificational Order: The Norwegian Experience', in G. Esping-Andersen (ed.) (1993).

LAND, H. (1994), 'The Demise of the Male Breadwinner', in Baldwin and Falkingham (eds.), *Social Security and Social Change* (London: Harvester Wheatsheaf).

LANE, C. (1993), 'Gender and the Labour Market in Europe: Britain, Germany and France Compared', *Sociological Review*, 41(2): 274–301.

LASLETT, P. (1983), *The World we Have Lost* (London: Methuen).

LE PRINCE, F. (1991), 'Day Care for Young Children in France', in Melhuish and Moss (eds.), *Day Care for Young Childern* (London: Tavistock/Routledge).

LEIRA, A. (1992), *Welfare States and Working Mothers* (Cambridge: Cambridge University Press).

—— (1993), 'The "women-friendly" Welfare State: The Case of Norway and Sweden', in J. Lewis (ed.) (1993).

—— (1994), 'Combining Work and Family: Working Mothers in Scandinavia and in the European Community', in P. Brown and R. Crompton (eds.), *A New Europe? Economic Restructuring and Social Exclusion* (London: UCL Press).

—— (1992), *Welfare States and Working Mothers* (Cambridge: Cambridge University Press).

LEWIS, J. (1993) (ed.), *Women and Social Policies in Europe* (Aldershot: Edward Elgar).

—— and ASTROM, G. (1992), 'Equality, Difference and State Welfare: Labor Market and Family Policies in Sweden', *Feminist Studies*, 18(1): 59–87.

—— (1980), *The Politics of Motherhood: Maternity and Child Welfare in England 1900–1939* (London: Croom Helm).

—— (1992), 'Gender and the Development of Welfare Regimes', *Journal of European Social Policy*, 2(3): 159–73.

LOWN, J. (1983), 'Not so much a Factory, More a Form of Patriarchy', in E. Gamarnikow, D. Morgan, J. Purvis, and D. Taylorson, *Gender, Class and Work*

(London: Heinemann).

LINDLEY, R. (1994) (ed.), *Labour Market Structures and Prospects for Women* (Manchester: Equal Opportunities Commission).

LISTER, R. (1992), 'Women, Economic Dependency and Citizenship', *Journal of Social Policy*, 19(4): 445–67.

LYOTARD, J. (1984), *The Postmodern Condition* (Manchester: Manchester University Press).

MARTIN, J., and ROBERTS, C. (1984), *Women and Employment: A Lifetime Perspective* (London: HMSO).

MAYNARD, M. (1994), 'Race, Gender and the Concept of "Difference" in Feminist Thought', in H. Afshar and M. Maynard (eds.), *The Dynamics of 'Race' and Gender* (London: Taylor and Francis).

—— (1995), 'Beyond the "Big Three": The Development of Feminist Theory into the 1990s', *Women's History Review*, 4(3): 259–81.

MORRIS, L. (1990), *The Workings of the Household* (Cambridge: Polity).

MOSS, P. (1991), 'Day Care for Young Children in the United Kingdom', in Melhuish and Moss (eds.), *Day Care for Young Children* (London: Tavistock/Routledge).

—— (1990), *Childcare in the European Community* (Brussels: Commission of the European Communities).

MOZNY, I. (1993), *The Czech Family in Transition from Social to Economic Capital* (Prague: CEU).

MYRDAL, A., and KLEIN, V. (1956), *Women's Two Roles* (London: Routledge and Kegan Paul).

O'CONNOR, J. (1993), 'Gender Class and Citizenship in the Comparative Analysis of Welfare State Regimes', *British Journal of Sociology*, 44/3: 501–18.

PAHL, J. (1983), 'The Allocation of Money and the Structuring of Inequality Within Marriage', *Sociological Review*, 31/2: 237–62.

—— (1989), *Money and Marriage* (London: Macmillan).

PAHL, R. (1995), *After Success* (Cambridge: Polity).

PAHL, R. E. (1984), *Divisions of Labour* (Oxford: Blackwell).

—— (1988) (ed.), *On Work* (Oxford: Blackwell).

PARSONS, T. (1949), 'The Social Structure of the Family', in R. Anshen (ed.), *The Family, its Functions and Destiny* (New York: Harper).

PATEMAN, C. (1988), *The Sexual Contract* (Cambridge: Polity).

—— (1989), 'The Patriarchal Welfare State', in C. Pateman (ed.), *The Disorder of Women* (Cambridge: Polity).

PERSSON, I. (1990), 'The Third Dimension', in I. Persson (ed.), *Generating Equality in the Welfare State* (Oslo: Norwegian University Press).

PHILLIPS, A., and Moss, P. (1988), *Who cares for Europe's Children?* (Brussels: EC).

PHIZACKLEA, A., and WOLKOWITZ, C. (1995), *Homeworking Women* (London: Sage).

PINCHBECK, I. (1981), *Women Workers and the Industrial Revolution* (London: Virago).

POLANYI, K. (1957), *The Great Transformation* (Boston: Beacon Press).

POLLERT, A. (1996), 'Gender and Class Revisited: or the Poverty of "Patriarchy"', *Sociology*, 30(4): 639–59.

PRINGLE, R. (1988), *Secretaries Talk: Sexuality, Power and Work* (London: Verso).

PURCELL, K. (1988), 'Gender and the Experience of Employment', in D. Gallie (ed.), *Employment in Britain* (Oxford: Blackwell).

RILEY, D. (1983), *War in the Nursery* (London: Virago).

ROETHLISBERGER, F. J., and DICKSON, W. J. (1947), *Management and the Worker* (Cambridge, Mass.: Harvard University Press).

ROWNTREE FOUNDATION (1995), *Inquiry into Income and Wealth* (York).

ROYAL SOCIETY OF ARTS (1996), *Towards a New Definition of Work* (London).

RUBERY, J. (ed.) (1988), *Women and Recession* (London: Routledge and Kegan Paul).

——and FAGAN, C. (1993), *Occupational Segregation of Women and Men in the European Community* (Brussels: EC).

——(1994), 'Occupational Segregation: Plus Ça Change?' in R. Lindley (ed.), *Labour Market Structures and Prospects for Women* (Manchester: Equal Opportunities Commission).

RUBERY, J., HORRELL, S., and BURCHELL, B. (1994), 'Part-Time Work and Gender Inequality in the Labour Market', in A. M. Scott (ed.), *Gender Segregation and Social Change* (Oxford: Oxford University Press).

SAVAGE, M., and WITZ, A. (eds.) (1992), *Gender and Bureaucracy* (Oxford: Blackwell).

SAVAGE, M. (1992), 'Women's Expertise, Men's Authority', in M. Savage and A. Witz (eds.), *Gender and Bureaucracy* (Oxford: Blackwell).

SCOTT, A. MCEWEN (ed.) (1994), *Gender Segregation and Social Change* (Oxford: Oxford University Press).

SCOTT, H. (1974), *Does Socialism Liberate Women?* (Boston: Beacon Press).

SCOTT, J. D., ALWIN, F. and BRAUN, M. (1996), 'Generational Changes in Gender-Role Attitudes: Britain in a Cross-National Perspective', *Sociology*, 30(3): 471–92.

SEIDLER, V. J. (1987), 'Reason, Desire and Male Sexuality', in P. Caplan (ed.), *The Cultural Construction of Sexuality* (London: Routledge).

SHORTER, E. (1976), 'Women's Work: What Difference did Capitalism Make?' *Theory and Society*, 3: 513–27.

SILTANEN, J. (1986), 'Domestic Responsibilities and the Structuring of Employment', in R. Crompton and M. Mann (eds.), *Gender and Stratification* (Cambridge: Polity).

SMITH, D. (1973), 'Women, the Family, and Corporate Capitalism', in M. Stephenson (ed.), *Women in Canada* (Toronto: New Press).

STACEY, M. (1981), 'The Division of Labour Revisited', in P. Abrams *et al.* (eds.), *Practice and Progress: British Sociology 1950–1980* (London: Allen & Unwin).

VEBLEN, T. (1934), *The Theory of the Leisure Class* (London: Modern Library).

VOGLER, C., and PAHL, J. (1993), 'Social and Economic Change and the Organisation of Money within Marriage', *Work, Employment and Society*, 7(1): 71–95.

References

WALBY, S. (1990), *Theorizing Patriarchy* (Oxford: Basil Blackwell).

—— (1986), *Patriarchy at Work* (Cambridge: Polity Press).

WARDE, A. and HETHERINGTON, K. (1993), 'A Changing Domestic Division of Labour?' *Work, Employment and Society,* 7(1): 23–45.

WATSON, G. (1994), 'The Flexible Workforce', *Employment Gazette* (July), 239–47.

WILSON, J. (ed.) (1993), *The Ghetto Underclass* (London: Sage).

WILSON, R. A. (1994), 'Sectoral and Occupational Change: Prospects for Women's Employment', in R. Lindley (ed.), *Labour Market Structures and Prospects for Women* (Manchester: Equal Opportunities Commission).

YOUNG, M., and WILMOTT, P. (1973), *The Symmetrical Family* (London: Routledge and Kegan Paul).

YUDKIN, S., and HOLME, A. (1963), *Working Mothers and their Children* (London: Michael Joseph).

Index

Index